EDUCATION, POLICY AND SOCIAL JUSTICE

Also available from Continuum

EDUCATION, POLICY AND SOCIAL JUSTICE

JUSTICE

Learning and Skills

James Avis

continuum

Continuum International Publishing Group

The Tower Building   80 Maiden Lane, Suite 704

11 York Road   New York, NY 10038

London

SE1 7NX

www.continuumbooks.com

© James Avis 2007

British Library Cataloguing-in-Publication Data

A catalogue record for this book is available from the British Library.

ISBN: 978-0-8264-8693-6 (paperback)

Library of Congress Cataloging-in-Publication Data

A catalog record for this book is available from the Library of Congress.

Typeset by Fakenham Photosetting Limited, Fakenham, Norfolk

Printed and bound in Great Britain by Biddles Ltd, King's Lynn, Norfolk

Contents

Acknowledgements

I am grateful to Taylor & Francis for allowing me to draw upon and rework previously published papers: 'Improvement through research: policy science or policy scholarship', in *Research in Post-compulsory Education*, vol. 11, no. 1, 2006, pp. 107–114; 'Beyond performativity: reflections on activist professionalism and the labour process', in *Journal of Education Policy*, vol. 20, no. 2, 2005, pp. 209–22; 'Work-based learning and social justice: learning to labour?', in *Journal of Education and Work*, vol. 17, no. 2, 2004, pp. 197–217; 'Re-thinking trust in a performative culture: the case of education', in *Journal of Education Policy*, vol. 18, no. 3, 2003, pp. 315–32; 'Imaginary friends: managerialism, globalisation and post-compulsory education and training in England', in *Discourse: Studies in the Cultural Politics of Education*, vol. 23, no. 1, 2002, pp. 75–90; 'Shifting identity – new conditions and the transformation of practice: teaching within post-compulsory education', in *Journal of Vocational Education and Training*, vol. 51, no. 2, 1999, pp. 245–64; 'From reproduction to learning culture', in *British Journal of Sociology of Education*, vol. 27, no. 3, 2006, pp. 341–54. www.tandf.co.uk

In particular Chapter 3 draws upon 'Work-based learning', Chapter 4 on 'From reproduction to learning culture' and Chapter 5, 'Shifting identity'.

1
Introduction

This introduction locates the ideational context within which post-compulsory education is placed. To begin with this chapter examines, albeit in a somewhat rhetorical fashion, the connections between education, the economy and social justice favoured by policy-makers – themes developed further in subsequent chapters. These connections have been iteratively present within state policy for much of the twentieth century and into the twenty-first. Although the relationship between education, economy and social justice is uneven and has been articulated differently at particular historical moments, there is nevertheless a common thread in the way in which these elements have been combined and understood. This understanding draws a clear association between a successful economy, social justice and an education system that develops the skill and knowledge base of the workforce. It is claimed that a successful economy is one which offers greater opportunity and therefore, in a fairly straightforward manner, is thought to contribute towards social justice, prosperity and social well-being.

In the West lifelong learning is thought to be the key to economic success. Competitiveness is to be pursued with the whole of society oriented towards this particular end, with all members of society developing subjective dispositions that align with this goal. They are to become enterprising subjects who possess the flexibility and adaptability needed to respond successfully to the ever changing economic and social conditions in which they are located. Competitive success in world markets, it is claimed, will not only offer economic benefits but also provide for social well-being, which in turn form the basis for social cohesion and inclusion. There is a happy coincidence, or at least so it is said, between the needs of capital, those who labour, other members of society and the state. We are all in effect seen as stakeholders who share a common interest in the ongoing success of the economy. A vibrant and dynamic economy is rhetorically construed as pivotal to the well-being of all.

These assertions are not new and the claims and demands that were placed on education throughout much of the twentieth century, becoming familiar themes following the end of the Second World War. What is new, however, in the current conjuncture is the urgency with which such claims are made and the manner in which they are set within a particular understanding of globalization, which is construed as an irresistible force. Globalization comes to be seen as a fact of economic life, one that has to be accommodated. Economic, education and social systems therefore need to adapt and respond appropriately to the consequences of globalization and its underpinning logic.

The result of these arguments for Britain, as for other Western economies, is that older forms of manufacturing which utilize low investment in both plant and the skills of the workforce come to be seen as no longer viable and will inevitably be relocated elsewhere in the global economic system. Such movements of jobs and plant should not be resisted but rather embraced and used as a stimulus to develop new skills within the labour force and to encourage a dynamic economy. To do otherwise would be to impede the social and economic development required to sustain a vibrant and successful economy on a global stage. Failure to respond creatively and dynamically to the demands of globalization would result in an economy trapped in redundant forms, leading to long-term social and economic decline.

Within this particular *zeitgeist* the role of the state is to facilitate global economic success and enable the workforce to develop new skills in order to add value to the products and services produced. Highly skilled workers who marshal their skills effectively in the labour process are seen as the route not only to global economic success but also to societal well-being. In the latter years of the twentieth century the association between the development of skilled workers in Western economies and economic competitiveness was understood in a relatively straightforward manner. The development of the skills base would bring with it value-added wage labour that would lead to competitive advantage. However, as we enter the twenty-first century the emerging economies of China and India, as with other similarly placed societies, are also investing in the development of skilled labour. In the West the response has been an intensification of the call for the development of value-added waged labour. There has however been scant concern for the impact of these developments upon social and economic relations. The logic of globalization, at least for policy-makers, dictates the route to competitiveness and the type of labour market and training strategies that should be adopted to produce the knowledgeable and skilled worker now required in the workplace. Such a worker is able to respond adaptively to the turbulent economic conditions that are now encountered, and is able to continually develop skills that contribute to value-added labour processes.

Throughout the post-war period education was seen as key not only for the development of skilled and knowledgeable workers but also as an important route to greater social and economic equality. It was hoped that providing more equitable educational opportunities would enable the upward mobility of disadvantaged groups, particularly in relation to class, gender and ethnicity/race. The manner in which this was to be accomplished varied according to the educational sector and period in which interventions were made. In the late 1960s and 1970s comprehensive schools were seen as vehicles to deliver greater opportunities for disadvantaged groups. However, with the advent of Thatcherism, and latterly New Labour, specialist schools, academies and colleges of various kinds have come to be seen as more suited to this goal. Yet despite variations in institutional forms there remains an overarching assumption that the economy demands ever increasing skills from its workforce and that this provides a dynamic towards greater equality. In other words the economy holds the promise of offering skilled, knowledgeable work with a resulting increase in wages, and in tandem with this claim rests the suggestion that correspondingly the demand for un- and semi-skilled labour will be reduced.

Echoes of meritocracy surround these arguments that suggest changes in the economy open up greater opportunities for all members of society. Economic changes aligned with the provision of educational opportunities that offer disadvantaged groups wider opportunities in this way contribute towards social justice. The interest in widening participation as well as the development of lifelong learning is rhetorically constructed as a means to this end. Sitting alongside this argument is the claim that whatever position we hold, whether it be in or out of work, with few or many skills or qualifications, there is a constant need to develop and acquire new skills. In such a context post-compulsory education and training (PCET) occupies an important place.

For those unfamiliar with English education it is useful to indicate briefly the way in which various terms are being used. One of the unfortunate characteristics of the English context is the plethora of terms surrounding education that can lead to confusion. The term PCET is being used in a fluid way. On one level it is being associated with colleges of further education (FE) in England, institutions that bear some resemblance to community colleges in the USA and with technical and further education colleges (TAFE) in Australia. Further education colleges in England have been concerned with vocational and technical education but they do much more than this, having an important role in 16–19 education, latterly provision for 14–19-year-olds, and also adult education. FE colleges are diverse institutions whose provision can range from basic skills to degree-level work. Colleges are marked by their particular histories as well as and relatedly the local and regional contexts in which they are placed (see Lucas, 2004). However, at the time of writing there is a state concern to clarify the role of further education as well as to wed it more firmly to meeting the needs of the economic system (Foster, 2005; LSC, 2005; DfES, 2006). In this book the term post-compulsory education and training is used as a generic term to describe the breadth of provision that is encompassed by the sector, regardless of institutional location. As a result of the funding arrangements deriving from the Learning and Skills Council (LSC), as well as the orientation of much of the sector towards vocational technical and skill development, it has been described as the learning and skills sector. This sector encompasses the range of provision provided within colleges of further education as well as that of other training providers.

The learning and skills sector and post-compulsory education and training are seen as playing a crucial role in the ongoing development of national competitiveness. It is anticipated that they will make a contribution to the development of skilled labour at craft and technician level, whether this is in service or other sectors of the economy. It is at this level that it is felt there is an inadequate supply of skilled labour (see Foster, 2005; Leitch, 2005; DfES, 2006). The education system is thought to be successful in developing highly skilled workers through higher education, but lower down it is considered to be much less successful. If the economy is to be successful, so it is claimed, these deficiencies need to be addressed and post-compulsory education and training are central to this project.

This book examines the global policy context within which PCET is placed. It explores the nature of the competitiveness education settlement, seeking to consider the limitations and possibilities that exist for progressive social and educative practice. Underpinning the current competitive settlement lies a particular construction of the economy and its place within globalization. This carries with it a particular role for education, namely to develop the forms of labour required by a globalized economy. How, within this context, is work imagined? A number of concepts have been used to describe the apparent shifts that have taken place in waged labour, amongst which we find Fordism, neo- and post-Fordism. The promise offered in the competitive settlement is that value-added waged labour provides the route to personally satisfying and creative work. These notions need to be deconstructed and set against alternative constructions of the economy and social relations. Whilst this is a theme that runs throughout the book it is a particular feature of Chapter 2, 'Fordism, post-Fordism and beyond', where these issues are addressed.

Chapter 2 examines the way in which employment and education are conceived in education policy, drawing upon the notion of settlement, Fordism and post-Fordism as well as constructions of the knowledge/information society. The latter discussion addresses questions of individualization, networks and the knowledge economy. The argument in this chapter is closely linked to an examination of the implications of the analysis for questions of social justice. Social justice is another thematic concern that is addressed throughout the book.

Chapter 3, 'Work-based learning and social justice', engages with a number of the arguments that were addressed in the preceding chapter. Work-based learning has been understood as a way in which economic competitiveness can be enhanced as well as a means of developing social cohesion and inclusion. This chapter explores debates concerned with work-based learning and considers them in relation to notions of knowledge and social capital. In particular it examines debates concerned with work-based learning and work-based knowledge, as well as the development of vocational pathways for the 14–19 age group. Policy-makers hope this pathway will provide a route for social inclusion by building upon the vocational interests of those young people who have become disaffected or disillusioned with school.

Chapter 4 'Learner dispositions: continuity and change', has two ambitions. First, to explore the lived experiences of students in further education, seeking to examine the empirical continuities and discontinuities in learner dispositions towards PCET. This is accompanied by an analysis of the way in which theorists have tried to make sense of these relations. The chapter reviews some of the early work that has addressed learner experience within PCET and sets this against more recent work. Throughout the chapter there is an interest in relating these theorizations to the socio-economic context from which they derive. The chapter concludes by returning to questions of social justice and the possibilities and limitations for the development of progressive practice, a theme returned to in Chapter 7.

There is a major paradox surrounding policy constructions of waged labour that emphasize the need for knowledgeable and skilled workers. Although post-Fordist work relations are construed as a developing feature of waged labour, teaching within PCET is marked by managerialist relations and the intensification of labour. Following the incorporation of colleges in the early 1990s after removal from local authority control, managerialist forms have become a dominant feature of labour relations within the sector. This has resulted in a loss of professional autonomy and control for teachers. Chapter 5, 'Teachers and the transformation of practice', explores the social and economic context of teaching within post-compulsory education. It examines the lived experiences of lecturers working in the sector and suggests that the attempt to explain these in terms of proletarianization or reprofessionalization is limited, arguing instead that we are witnessing a transformation of teaching and learning that opens up new forms of practice and identities for lecturers. As with the earlier discussion running through the book the progressive possibilities as well as limitations that reside are examined, in this case specifically those of new work relations within further education. The analysis in this chapter can be set alongside that of Chapter 4, which examined student orientations and formative processes in relation to class, race and gender, alluded to in Chapter 3.

Chapter 6, 'Knowledge, curriculum and power', draws upon the earlier analysis exploring the construction of knowledge and the curriculum in PCET, seeking to relate these to questions of power. It engages with discussions of socially situated learning and the manner in which this is articulated to the production of knowledge. The chapter explores conceptualizations of the curriculum 'as fact' and 'as practice', as well as the orientations of public educators and industrial trainers towards knowledge. It similarly relates processual understandings of the curriculum to social realist models of knowledge. The chapter explores the limits and possibilities of the curricular frameworks within which post-compulsory education is placed. The analysis anticipates the arguments developed in Chapter 7 that call for an expansive notion of practice which extends beyond the classroom into the wider social formation.

Chapter 7, 'Social justice, post-compulsory education and practice', explores a tension between an interest in social justice and the ongoing improvement of practice. To address this it examines two rather different types of literature. First, early policy documents that address post-compulsory education and second, current debates concerned with educational research and critiques forwarded by the state and other commentators which suggest that educational research has not engaged sufficiently with practice and has therefore failed to make any significant impact upon learning and teaching. The concluding sections of the chapter explore the notion of practice, returning to the *Transforming Learning Cultures (TLC) project* that was discussed in Chapter 4 and in addition considers the work of Lingaard *et al.* (2003a, b). This discussion seeks to explore the notion of practice and set this alongside an expansive understanding that locates practice within its wider socio-economic context.

Chapter 8, 'Conclusion', draws together the main arguments of the book. This is followed by an examination of current debates that call for a policy emphasis upon the development of 'well-being'. This debate seeks to respond to the social costs of neo-liberal economic policies and contains both possibilities and limitations for radical practice. It can however, in Gramsci's terms, easily sit with passive revolution that secures the interest of capital.

2
Fordism, post-Fordism and beyond

This chapter explores a number of issues that address the ways in which employment and education are conceived in policy and practice. A useful way to examine these issues is through the notion of settlement and the discursive shifts in the way in which the economy and economic relations have been understood in the post-war period and the early years of this century. This latter theme entails an examination of Fordism and post-Fordism followed by an analysis of constructions of the knowledge/information society. A common theme throughout this chapter concerns questions of social justice and the construction of learners, economy and skill.

The competitiveness settlement

It has almost become a cliché to talk of a settlement or new consensus formed around education in general and post-compulsory education in particular, whereby schooling is to be closely aligned with the needs of employers. Throughout much of the second half of the twentieth century education systems have been criticized for their failure to produce the forms of labour required by capital. Although this criticism has been applied with some vehemence to English education, it has also been the case elsewhere. For example, US education has been similarly castigated for its failings, as have from time to time many European systems (Apple, 2001, 2004; Aronowitz and Giroux, 1986; Giroux, 1992; Leitch, 2005).

As we enter the early years of the twenty-first century the association between education and employability seems to have become embedded within educational policy discourse, as well as more popular understandings of the purposes of education. Consequently there has been the formation of a generalized consensus surrounding education. This consensus is not all of a piece, being fractured in various ways, but is one that attempts to hold together a diverse range of constituents – employers, young people, parents and so on – having differing and potentially conflicting interests. The Gramscian notion of settlement addresses these issues and points towards processes that are concerned with the ongoing formation of a generalized common sense that aligns with the needs of capital.

By settlement I have in mind a generally agreed framework, or set of assumptions, surrounding the nature and development of education in general and post-compulsory education and training in particular, as well as, crucially, their relation to the economic system (see Avis, 1993, 1996a, 2002; Avis *et al.*, 1996). Educational settlements seek to 'organize' a range of constituents from educationalists through to industrialists, and in addition attempt to take on board the interests of ordinary people in their own economic well-being and that of their children. Settlements seek to organize common sense in a manner that is compatible with the interests of capital. In the case of post-compulsory education elements of the current settlement have been present for some time and have centred upon a shared analysis of the failings of the English economy and its education system. For a number of years the English economy has been castigated for its short termism and lack of investment in training and education (Hutton, 1995, 1997). At the same time the education system has been criticized for its elitism and failure to encourage mass participation in post-compulsory education and training, initially in relation to further and latterly to higher education (see Ainley, 2005a, b; DfEE, 1998a, b; Kennedy, 1997).

What is useful about the notion of settlement, coming as it does out of Gramscian Marxism, is its ability to take on board contradiction, tension and negotiation as well as an awareness of the fragility of settlements (see Education Group II, 1991). The notion of settlement embodies a recognition of attempts to create a social bloc or alliance around education through which the interests of capital are secured. Stuart Hall, writing on Thatcherism, comments:

> The whole project of Thatcherism as a form of politics has been to construct a new social bloc, and in this project ideology is critical. A social bloc is, by definition, not homogeneous. It does not consist of one whole class or even part of one class. It has to be constructed out of groups, which are very different in terms of their material interests and social positions. The question is, can these differences of position and interests be constructed into a 'unity'? (It never is a unity, in the strict sense.) Can these diverse identities be welded together into a 'collective will'? (1988, p. 262)

Although the Thatcherite project failed to construct such a social bloc, it did succeed in constituting the framework upon which subsequent educational and economic policies were developed. Thatcherism promulgated the construction of a common sense in which 'there is no alternative' but to accept the existence of a market-driven competitive capitalism.

The idea of hegemony sits alongside that of settlement and refers to the organization of consent whereby members of society recognize that there is no alternative but to accept the current economic arrangements. This ensures that the ability of capital to secure its interests is sustained. The notion of settlement refers to similar processes taking place in relation to education.

> Hegemony involves securing both the conditions for future capitalist production and the consent of the subordinated population to the social and cultural implications of 'progress'. It is exercised not only through law and coercion, but also through 'educative' processes in a larger sense, including schooling, the media and centrally political parties. It necessitates the building of new alliances that may be active

in promoting new solutions. Hegemony is not uniquely a product of 'the state' but involves the institutions of 'civil society' too.

If hegemony refers to the overall relations of force in a society, we wish to use the term educational settlement to refer to the balance of forces in and over schooling. Settlements entail at this 'regional level' rather than 'global level' some more or less enduring set of solutions to capital's educational needs, the putting together of a dominant alliance of forces, and a more widespread recruitment of popular support or inducement of popular indifference. (Education Group, 1981, p. 32)

It is important to recognize the vulnerability of hegemonic arrangements to challenge, as well as having an awareness that not all members of society will necessarily accept these arrangements as just or valid. However the point is that whilst we may challenge and contest these ideas they secure their power through the production of a common sense which claims there is no alternative. The Blairite interpretation of globalization would be a case in point. Here it is claimed we have no choice but to accept the reality of global economic competition and adjust our economic and education systems, as well as our individual orientations to paid labour, in line with this reality. Richard Johnson captures these ideas well when he writes:

The hegemonic is not necessarily what everyone *practices*, nor what everyone *believes in*. Hegemony is *not* dominant ideology saturating the whole formation; winning consent is not necessarily agreement. Rather the hegemonic is that for which *'there is no alternative'*. [My emphasis] (1998, p. 90)

Similarly Ann-Marie Smith reminds us:

A hegemonic project does not dominate political subjects: it does not reduce political subjects to pure obedience and it does not even require their unequivocal support for its specific demands. It pursues, instead, a far more subtle goal, namely the vision of the social order as the social order itself.

To describe a political project as hegemonic, then, is not to say that a majority of the electorate explicitly supports its policies, but to say that there appears to be no other alternative to this project's vision of society. (1994, p. 37)

These notions of hegemony and settlement carry with them contestation, renegotiation and iterative processes that attempt to constitute and reorganize forms of common sense to align with capitalist interests. Forms of opposition and contestation will inevitably remain but their visibility will be dependent upon the balance of force existing at the time. Implicit within conceptualizations of hegemony is an interest in securing the long-term goals of capital. This means that at particular moments concessions will be given to oppositional forces. Such a process is reflected in the post-war social democratic settlement with concessions being won by the working class in relation to the welfare state, commitment to full employment and so on. However, as a consequence of economic changes these concessions have been reined back and more oppressive forms of neo-liberal social relations have been put in place, albeit New Labour has attempted to mitigate the harshness of these relations by introducing a concern with social inclusion and cohesion (DfEE, 1998a, b; DfES, 2005a, b). Lawton (2005) discusses the tension within the Labour Party between an ethical socialism concerned with social justice and a Fabianism oriented towards economic efficiency. However in the current period this tension has been resolved through the dominance and acceptance of capitalist and globalized economic relations for which it is held, 'there is no alternative'.

The key focus of this chapter is upon the relationship between education and economic relations and thus far the discussion of settlement has been lodged within a capitalist logic. However, it is important to recognize the limitations of such a position before returning to a discussion of the economic and educational nexus. The Gramscian notion of hegemony and the utilization of this framework by the Education Group (1981) to formulate the notion of educational settlement that was drawn upon earlier, carries with it a number of tensions. Hegemony is rooted within a capitalist logic that prioritizes class at the expense of other social relations. Race and gender are marginalized and treated as epiphenomena of class relations and although the fragility of settlements is recognized there is a tendency to underplay this, at least until the ascendancy of Thatcherism. Although the following discussion focuses upon economic and therefore class relations, it is important to recognize that whilst analytically we can separate relations of class from those of gender and race, in practice they are intertwined. We are all positioned in relation to our class, gender, ethnicity, sexuality and so on, at particular points of time one or other of these may become prioritized and provide the lens through which the others are made sense of. In addition educational settlements may be accented differentially as a result of the way in which they are placed within particular educational locales and settings. The manner of New Labour's social justice agenda and the way in which this is presumed to facilitate economic success will be accented in various ways. For example, social justice concerns to do with inclusion and social participation will be stressed in relation to adult education whereas in other settings a greater stress may be placed upon the economic. It must be noted that within this ideational frame whatever the context at root the needs of capital and the economy are placed in a dominant position.

Fordism and post-Fordism

The social democratic settlement that was in place following the Second World War became increasingly vulnerable in the late 1960s and was finally superseded by Thatcherism in the 1970s. Underpinning the social democratic settlement were a number of elements – full employment, universal welfare provision as well as a meritocratic view of education that rested upon a desire to provide equal educational opportunities. This latter concern was expressed in the Labour Party's commitment to comprehensive education, albeit unevenly enacted (Lawton, 2005).

Paradoxically, this social democratic period following the Second World War was one in which Fordist work relations were pervasive. Braverman, writing in 1974, appropriated Marx's analysis of capital suggesting with the passage of time work would become increasingly degraded and the division between mental and manual labour would be exacerbated. The progressive deskilling of labour occurred for Braverman not only in traditional craft and manufacturing, but was also present amongst white-collar labour employed in offices and shops, as well as in many quasi-professional contexts. There are however a number of problems surrounding Braverman's work, not least of which is his tendency to treat as all of a piece changes effecting the labour process. This means that he is unable to address the manner in which deskilling in some areas of work may be accompanied by up- or reskilling in others. The model of the craft worker is somewhat roman-ticized, with gendered processes in the construction of, as well as the struggle over, skill being downplayed. In addition social processes and allied struggles that take place between labour and capital, the outcome of which leads to the social construction of skill, are similarly marginalized. This is because deskilling is seen as an endemic feature of capitalism. It is important to recognize that the notion of skill in part reflects the power of workers to define their work in such terms, and importantly, have it accepted as such. The very plasticity of the notion of skill can be seen currently in the way in which the term has been re-worked to take on dispositional features (see Warhurst *et al.*, 2004). We only need to reflect on the impor-tance given to personal and transferable skills in contemporary policy discourse to see a reflection of this process. These ideas are sometimes glossed over in notions of employability as well as in the aesthetics of labour, whereby personal attributes to do with sexuality and appearance have become transmogrified into skill (DfES, 2005b; Nickson *et al.*, 2001; Warhurst *et al.*, 2004).

Fordist work relations can be seen as embodied within mass production in the early years of the twentieth century, a model that continued until human labour became increasingly marginalized through the introduction of robotization in the West. However it is important to recognize that such relations continue to characterize much paid labour in Western economies. Fordist work relations have a number of characteristics, being marked by a detailed division of labour carrying with it low skill, low trust as well as relatively low wages. In Fordism there is a notable division between conception of the labour process and its execution. In a number of respects Fordist work relations derive from Fredrick Taylor's scientific management that carried with it a concern to tightly surveil and define the labour process. These types of work relations were closely aligned with the period of social democracy following the end of the Second World War. Whilst Fordist work relations are based on low trust and low skills the protected nature of the British economy and utilization of Keynesian economics meant that in international terms British workers, and indeed those working in similar conditions in the USA and elsewhere, were relatively well paid during this period. This was the basis upon which the social democratic settlement was built (see for example the affluent workers studies, Goldthorpe *et al.*, 1968a, b, 1969). The relative affluence of such groups of workers has subsequently been undercut as a consequence of de-industrialization, the impact of globalization and the shift in the balance of power away from waged labour to capital.

The collapse of the social democratic settlement and the ascendancy of Thatcherism in the late 1970s and 1980s carried with it a commitment to neo-liberalism, the market and the desire to put in place increasingly competitive relations. Keynesian economic policy and a protected market used to sustain relatively high wages and the welfare state came to be seen as no longer a viable option. In addition, work relations based upon low trust and low skill came to be seen as antithetical to securing competitive advantage in a globalized economy. Finegold and Soskice (1988), in their seminal work, argued that the British and in particular the English economy was trapped within a low skills equilibrium, one that perversely offered benefits to employers, young people and their families, but which was detrimental to the economy in the long run.

They argued that steps should be taken to move the economy towards work relations based upon high trust, high skill and therefore high wages. Such an economy it was claimed would be able to secure the social and economic well-being of the society – the alternative was to face secular decline with a falling standard of living and ongoing retrenchment of the welfare state. Not dissimilar arguments were forwarded by Sir Christopher Ball who called for a shift away from a vicious circle based upon low skills and low wages to a virtuous circle predicated upon high skills and high wages (Ball, 1991, p. 2). These arguments sit alongside those that celebrate the possibilities which lie within post-Fordist work relations. Table 2.1 utilizes Lauder and Brown's description of Fordism and post-Fordism.

At the time it was unclear whether these post-Fordist ideas were prefiguratively describing the economy in a somewhat deterministic manner or whether this was felt to be the direction that should be pursued to ensure a vibrant economy and a steadily increasing standard of living for all. The Finegold and Soskice paper seemed to imply that there was no question but to follow the high-skills route as the alternative would result in societal and economic decline. And indeed when Brown and Lauder were writing in the early 1990s, post-Fordist work relations seemed to offer not only higher wages but also higher levels of job satisfaction. Post-Fordist work relations seemed to offer a way out of the forms of exploitation and oppression that had previously surrounded waged labour.

Analyses such as those of Braverman (1974), which had been informed by Marxism and had pointed towards the ongoing degradation of work, now seemed out of place and to have been superseded by the new economic conditions in which work was placed. A new epoch was on the horizon in which previous patterns of class struggle would be transcended. This was the ideational context that third-way politics was able to occupy, which suggested the division between left and right had been transcended – ideas that served to underpin Blairite politics. Giddens comments:

Table 2.1 Characteristics of Fordism and post-Fordism

Fordism	Post-Fordism
Economy, competition and production process	
Protected national markets	Global competition
Mass production of standardized products	Flexible production systems/small batch/niche markets
Bureaucratic hierarchical organizations	Flatter and flexible organizational structures
Compete by full capacity utilization and cost cutting	Compete by innovation diversification, sub-contracting
Labour	
Fragmented and standardized work tasks	Flexible specialization/multi-skilled workers
Low-trust/low-discretion majority employed in manufacturing sector/blue-collar jobs	High-trust/high-discretion majority employed in service sector/white-collar jobs
Little on-the-job training, little formal training required for most jobs	Regular on-the-job training, greater demand for knowledgeable workers
Small managerial and professional elite	Growing managerial and professional service/class
Fairly predictable labour market histories	Unpredictable labour market histories due to technological change and increased economic uncertainty
Politics and ideology	
Trade union solidarity	Decline in trade union membership
Class-based political affiliation	Declining significance of class-based politics
Importance of locality/class/gender-based lifestyles	Fragmentation and pluralism global village
Mass consumption of consumer durables	Individualized consumption/Consumer choice

Source: Brown and Lauder, 1992, Table 1.1 p. 4.

The third way is an attempt to resolve the key problem of the time I think, which is how to create a dynamic economy which still has some measure of social solidarity and social justice in it. Thatcherism is essentially exhausted, you can't run the world as though it was just a market place and the Keynesian old left has become in some part obsolete. (Analysis, 1998, p. 3)

[The] 'third way' refers to a framework of thinking and policy making that seeks to adapt social democracy to a world which has changed fundamentally over the past two or three decades. It is a third way in the sense that it is an attempt to transcend both old style social democracy and neoliberalism. (Giddens, 1998, p. 26)

Post-Fordist arguments resonated with educational policy rhetoric. Indeed throughout the twentieth century state education policy documents had drawn upon the rhetoric of an ever increasing demand for ever higher levels of skill amongst the workforce. This in turn was echoed in the arguments of policy-makers whereby the interests of employers, young people and their parents as well as wider society could all be brought into alignment. All members of society were seen as having a common interest in the ongoing success of the economy, with education being seen as pivotal to achieving societal well-being (see DfES, 2006). The Internet summary of New Labour's 1998 white paper, *The Learning Age: A New Renaissance for a New Britain,* stated:

Why learning matters
For *individuals,* **learning will help everyone acquire the new skills and qualifications needed for employment and advancement. Learning will increase our earning power**. In addition it will help older people to stay healthy and active, strengthen families and the wider community and encourage independence. Opportunities to learn will lead us to greater appreciation of art, music, poetry and literature, and develop our potential as rounded human beings.

For *businesses,* **learning will help them to be more successful by adding value and keeping them up-to-date. Learning will develop the human and intellectual capital which is now at the centre of a nation's competitive strength. It will provide the tools to manage industrial and technological change, and help generate ideas, research and innovation on which economic progress relies. As productivity depends on the whole workforce, we must invest in everyone**.

For *the nation,* **learning will be the key to a strong economy and an inclusive society**. It will offer a way out of dependency and low expectation towards self-reliance and self-confidence. In doing so, it will be at the heart of the Government's welfare reform programme. We must bridge the 'learning divide' which blights so many communities and the widening gap, in terms of employment expectations and income, between those who have benefited from education and training and those who have not. [My emphasis in bold] (DfEE, 1998a, unnumbered)

In part interventions such as these seek to construct a common-sense understanding of the relationship between these constituencies, one that is set within a context that accepts unquestioningly capitalist relations and where we all share a common interest in economic success. Ultimately, we are all on the same side, older forms of social and class antagonism having been transcended by the *new times* in which we find ourselves. Where difficulties arise these are residues of the past and so can be readily overcome. However, to be competitive in a globalized economy necessitates developing society's potential to the full. Human and social capital needs to be fully developed so that economic success, whilst never assured, becomes increasingly likely. Ideas such as these underpin meritocratic understandings of education, they provide support for equal opportunities policy that seeks to maximize the potential of disadvantaged groups. Tony Blair's commitment to an opportunity society reflects this position (Blair, 2004a; and see Labour Party, 2004). For New Labour such strategies are central to its project of social cohesion and inclusion and also to its variant of a social justice agenda. Education for all comes to be seen as a vehicle to maximize individual potential, no matter what the social background or individual starting point. Concurrently education for all and skill development is seen to contribute towards national competitiveness (Leitch, 2005). David Blunket, the then secretary of state for education, writes in his foreword to *Excellence in Schools*:

We want to change attitudes towards education and foster a reali-sation that education matters to everyone.

To overcome economic and social disadvantage and to make equality of opportunity a reality, we must strive to eliminate, and never excuse underachievement in the most deprived parts of our country. Educational attainment encourages aspiration and self belief in the next generation, and it is through family learning, as well as scholarship through formal schooling that success will come.

We are talking about investing in human capital in the age of knowledge. To compete in the global economy, to live in a civilised society and to develop the talents of each and every one of us, we will have to unlock the potential of every young person. By doing so, each can flourish, building on their own strengths and developing their own special talents. We must overcome the spiral of disadvantage, in which alienation from or failure within the education system is passed from one generation to the next. (DfEE, 1997, p. 3)

Employers through their input are to play a central part in the development of the education system, becoming a key element in the framework through which learners acquire 'useful knowledge'. The white papers *14–19 Education and Skill* and *Skills: Getting on in Business, Getting on at Work*, reflect the importance placed on employer input. The first acknowledges the importance of employers in the development of vocational pathways and the second, their role in lifelong learning (DfES, 2005a, b). These themes have been brought together in the 2006 white paper *Further Education: Raising Skills, Improving Life Chances*, which describes these two concerns as:

Urgent requirements – a transformation of the life chances of young people and the skills of the workforce – are the drivers for the reforms set out in this white paper. (DfES 2006, p. 17)

These reforms focus on the needs of the economy, and particularly those of employers. Even though the needs of learners are set alongside those of employers the latter are placed in a dominant position. Ironically, English employers in particular have not been overly concerned with education and training, though there are some notable exceptions. Training has been generally considered to be an expense rather than an investment in the future (Finegold and Soskice, 1988; Hyland, 1994; Unwin and Wellington, 2001; and see Rikowski, 2001).

Over the past 20 years or so we find within the policy documents a rhetorical move towards an economy characterized by high skills, high trust, high-waged work relations – an economy in which the skill and knowledge of the worker become pivotal to economic success. In this scenario the worker/learner is construed not only as the route to competitiveness but is at the same time required to be infinitely flexible and adaptable, responding rapidly to the caprice of the economy. In this way the worker/learner will be required to reinvent themselves continuously so as to sustain employability. Cynically, Levitas notes:

> What is described as a 'lifetime entitlement to learning' is effectively a lifetime obligation to acquire and maintain marketable skills. (1999, p. 121)

Within the competitiveness settlement the worker is seen as the key factor of production and economic success, which arises through the application of value-added waged labour.

Central to the competitiveness settlement is the rhetorical claim that if the English economy is to compete globally it needs to ensure that the labour force is highly skilled and educated in order to generate value-added products. Failure to do so, it is claimed, will lead to secular economic and social decline. These arguments are predicated on the need to break away from the low-skills equilibrium and to replace it with one based upon high-skill, high trust and high-waged work relations (see Finegold and Soskice, 1988; and, for discussion, Coleman and Keep, 2001). These moves derive from an economic analysis which argues that there is a need to break away from the forms of Fordism characteristic of the post-war period and suggests we are now entering an epoch in which worker creativity is the key to economic success.

Such expectations have been furthered by analyses of the social formation that suggest we are moving into a qualitatively different economic and work context and that in this new epoch older forms of class antagonism have been superseded. It is here that we encounter discussions of reflexive modernization as well as New Labour's third way (see for discussion Avis, 2002). These arguments suggest that failure of the English economy to modernize in line with new conditions will lead to economic decline and a lowering of the standard of living – hence the need to break free of the low-skills equilibrium.

The policy rhetoric surrounding the competitiveness settlement ignores or plays down the presence of unskilled and semi-skilled jobs, which nevertheless remain central to the economy and to many people's working lives. Alison Wolf writes:

> Manufacturing jobs have declined ... However, this is far from meaning that there are fewer and fewer jobs for the unskilled because the labour market is demanding only skilled labour. On the contrary, the percentage of jobs which fall into the 'skilled crafts' categories has fallen steadily throughout the 1980s and 1990s, and is projected to decline yet more. Meanwhile, some occupations are thriving which require much less of a 'knowledge base'. The single fastest-growing job in the 1980s was 'postman'; that of the 1990s looks like being 'care assistant' in nursing homes and hospitals ... While professional and managerial jobs have certainly exploded in numbers, the greatest shrinkage has been among the skilled and semi-skilled manual jobs in the middle. Low-skilled openings still exist in their millions for people to do things like cleaning streets and offices, packing and delivering boxes, staffing call centres, or operating supermarket checkouts. (2002, pp. 48–9)

Anyon (2005) develops a similar analysis for the USA (and see Barry, 2005; Sennett, 2006):

> Most job openings in the next 10 years will not require either sophisticated skills or a college degree ... Most will require on-the-job training only, and will not require a college education; most will be in service and retail, where poverty-zone wages are the norm. (p. 20)

Even the Leitch review of skills, a report commissioned by the British state, which held a bullish view of skill and construed the ongoing skill development of the workforce as the route to competitiveness, conceded:

> These shifts in the type of jobs mean that changes in the labour market are not as simple as increased demand at the top end at the expense of jobs at the low-skill end. Work may instead be polarising

with the increase in the proportion of high-skilled workers leading to increased demand for less-skilled workers in some service jobs, but with technology increasingly substituting for intermediate-skill jobs. (2005, p. 29)

However, the neglect of the significance of un-skilled and semi-skilled jobs in the economy is compounded by the assumption that high-skilled work is the only route to competitiveness. Ewart Keep (1997, 1999; and see Warhurst *et al.*, 2004) has frequently drawn attention to the various routes to competitive advantage – the high-skills option being but one of these.

Skills are by no means the only, or even the most attractive route to competitive success, perhaps particularly so in the Anglo-Saxon world. Rather than seeing skill as THE key to competitive success, it might be more realistic to view upskilling as simply one model vying for senior managers' attention in a marketplace for ideas. There are many other competing models available. (Coleman and Keep, 2001, unnumbered)

There is no necessary economic or social imperative compelling employers to adopt the high-skill route. In addition a number of factors impinge on the labour process strategy developed by a particular firm, against which different routes to competitive advantage will be evaluated.

A discussion allied to skill and competitive advantage examines core organizational competences. Core competences refer to the characteristics of an organization that enable its success, allowing it to do things better or differently to its competitors (Coleman and Keep, 2001). These core competences can be concentrated within a particular part of the organization or more widely diffused. One can compare firms such as Aldi or Kwik Save that have relatively concentrated core competences against other organizations in which these are more widely diffused. Consequently the distribution of skill will in part be dependent on the strategy adopted towards these competences within particular organizations. This discussion indicates the complexity of work relations and counters the rhetorical claim that there is but one route to competitiveness – the high skills. There are a range of factors and processes that have a bearing on the way in which firms address these issues. Amongst these will be the product market, the form of competitive relations facing the firm, whether it be focused on price or quality, the pattern of industrial relations, its global and regional strategy and its orientation towards investment, along with many other factors. Brown reminds us:

> In many sectors of the economy, employers are reluctant to invest in new technologies or to upgrade the skills of the workforce, *recognising that it is still possible to make good profits through competition on price rather* than product or service innovation. [My emphasis] (2001, p. 248–9)

Brown *et al.* (2001) in *High Skills* draw our attention to the specific characteristics of the English route to competitiveness and the nature of its economy, split between a small high-skilled segment and a much larger low-skilled one. This economy is characterized by a low-skills/high-skills model, that is to say there is a polarization between a high-skilled segment of the labour market, an example of which would be bio-technology, set alongside a significant low-skilled sector. Other authors, reflecting this polarization, have described the labour market as being akin to an hourglass (Tomorrow project, undated).

A large low-skilled/low-waged sector in an economy impacts on product markets, encouraging competition on the basis of price rather than quality (see Hutton, 1995). Where competition is based on quality high-skilled work relations will be encouraged, whereas if price is paramount this is not the case. Mass markets based on price competition undermine the development of a high-skills economy.

> There are both demand and supply side-effects to having large numbers of workers on low wages or in poverty. With respect to the demand side ... both Hutton (1995) and Keep (1999) have argued that with so many workers on low wages it is hardly surprising that firms' dominant strategy has been to compete on price rather than quality, simply because the latter cannot be afforded. (Lauder, 2001, p. 196)

Gleeson and Keep (2004) remind us that for senior management, skills are 'a third or fourth order issue rather than a first order issue' (p. 57) and 'often incidental, to the achievement of organisational goals [the pursuit of profit]' (p. 45). Finally, the assumption that education is pivotal to the development of value-added labour by securing competitive advantage, requires qualification. Many nations seek to develop the skills and abilities of their workforce in order to gain a competitive edge, not all of whom will be successful in this endeavour or be in a position or even desire to pay higher wages. The outsourcing of HSBC's call centres to the Far East serves as an example. Not only is it suggested that Indian labour costs would stand at £1,200 p.a. for a call centre operative as against £12,000 p.a. in the UK, but that Indian operatives would not only be cheaper but more skilled and better qualified (Channel 4, 2003; Griffiths, 2003; White, 2003). However, these caveats need to be set within a globalized economic system, one marked by higher levels of openness than those of previous epochs. Or to put it another way, the world economic system now impacts upon the British economy in a way that is reminiscent of the manner in which it did upon the third world and developing nations in the past. Forms of insecurity and vulnerability that once faced the third world and developing countries are to a lesser extent echoed in Western economies.

These arguments illustrate the deeply misleading nature of the rhetorical construction of the economy and skills requirement present within the dominant policy discourse as well as the way in which these arguments are drawn upon in educational policy. Low-skilled, low-waged work remains a reality for large numbers of the working population. These wage relations encourage market competition on price rather than quality, which in the case of the latter would serve to develop the skills of the workforce. In addition the policy rhetoric ignores, or at least plays down, the different routes that can be pursued to gain competitive advantage, and the continued importance of low-skilled, low-waged work to the economy. Indeed the policy rhetoric is at best partial and at worst fraudulent. It is certainly ideologically driven and firmly located within capitalist interests.

Individualization, networks and the knowledge information society

It is commonplace amongst policy-makers to see education as pivotal to societal and economic well-being. This association transcends the particularities of specific social formations and forms a widely held belief, becoming a bulwark of an uncritically accepted common sense. Within the UK, and in particular England, a series of claims and assumptions are made about education and what it can deliver. If competitiveness is to be attained it is claimed that this will depend upon the education system producing highly skilled, flexible and adaptable workers – those able to contribute towards the production of value-added products. It would be as a result of the capacities and skills of the worker that competitive advantage would be secured. All sorts of other associations are linked to these claims – improved levels of job satisfaction, generalized upskilling, societal and economic well-being and so on. Thus the assumed link between having a degree and enhanced earning power is used by the current Labour government to justify charging fees and providing loans that are to be repaid from enhanced lifetime earnings (see for example, Hodge, 2003). Clear trends are in place that emphasize the relationship between the individual and their rights and responsibilities, one of which is to invest in themselves as human capital. These trends can be set against earlier Fordist epochs and forms of collective employment that characterized the immediate post-war period. The labour market has become increasingly fragmented and individualized. The employee has to be prepared to continuously develop themselves in order to gain and sustain employment. Callinicos cites Bourdieu (1998) approvingly:

'the *deterritorialization of the enterprise'* now freed from any specific attachment to region and nation – has ensured that 'insecurity is everywhere today'; '[o]bjective insecurity supports a generalized subjective insecurity which today affects, at the heart of an advanced economy, the majority of workers and even those who are not yet directly hit.' Indeed, this is part of 'a *mode of domination* of a new type, based on the institution of a generalized and permanent condition of insecurity aiming to compel the workers to submission, to the acceptance of exploitation'. (1999, p. 89)

Crudely, in the 1950s and 1960s, the relationship between education, employment and economy could be understood through the lens of reproduction. In particular the mass failure of the working class (as mediated through race and gender) could be seen as a response to the requirements of the economic system for un-skilled and semi-skilled labour (see for example, Brown, 1987; Willis, 1977). Such an analysis was equally appropriate to Western Europe and the USA (Bowles and Gintis, 1976). However, de-industrialization and globalization, as well as changes in the labour market, have unpicked these relations (Gleeson and Keep, 2004). Themes surrounding competitiveness have reconfigured the relation between education, employment and economy, providing a spin that centres upon the individual.

New Labour has accepted an economic model of the economy and social relations founded upon the competitiveness settlement. Labour's particular contribution has been to introduce an interest in social inclusion and cohesion to those of value-added waged labour and human capital. However the former interests remain predicated upon an economic logic whereby a socially inclusive and cohesive society would provide the stability required for economic success. In addition it offers the possibility to develop talent, skill and ability that would otherwise be overlooked to the detriment of society and the economy. It is at this juncture that Labour's interest in social capital arises, as well as the associated concern with regional and local regeneration. Although social capital antici-pates collective relations, it is nevertheless couched within an individualized framework (see Avis, 2003). Through the development of social networks and relations of trust the individual will be better placed to acquire information that will lead to waged work. Social networks enable the individual to draw upon community resources that facilitate entry to work and develop skills which enhance employability. Yet at the same time the way in which the collective is conceived is truncated, with the connection between the regional, local and wider structural relations being played down. This leads to an analysis that focuses upon the individual and the cultural, often moving towards suggestions of pathology. The local community may hold values that are antithetical to waged employment and which require interruption to generate individual employability. Or in a similar vein, the individual may have failed to develop the social skills that employers require, necessitating interventions so that they may acquire the appropriate and desired dispositions for waged labour.

The competitiveness discourse in its various manifestations places the individual learner at the centre. Developing the skills and capabilities of such an individual secures economic advantage as a result of value-added waged labour. Through their knowledge and skill the individual can generate value, thereby enhancing the product.

In Britain the state's response has been to place on the individual the responsibility of developing themselves as flexible and adaptable workers who can ride out and respond appropriately to such challenges. We see the emergence of the responsible individual. However as Olssen (and see Olssen, *et al.*, 2004) reminds us, this individual is one formed and constructed by the state:

In the shift from classical liberalism to neo-liberalism, then there is a new element added, for such a shift involved a change in subject position from 'homo economicus', who naturally behaves out of self interest and is relatively detached from the state, to 'manipulatable man', who is created by the state and who is continually encouraged to be 'perpetually responsive'. It is not that the conception of the self-interested subject is replaced or done away with by the new ideals of 'neo-liberalism', but that in an age of universal welfare the perceived possibilities of slothful indolence create necessities for new forms of vigilance, surveillance, performance appraisal and of forms of control generally. In this new model, the state has taken it upon itself to keep all up to the mark. (2003, pp. 199–200)

Within this policy context lies a very particular understanding of social relations. The notion of class as a relatively fixed social structure has been unpicked; instead we are offered a far more fluid and undetermined model of the social formation. The emphasis upon the individual and their agency is heightened in this ideational context. Even when structural phenomena are intimated at, the move is towards disadvantage and individual pathology. Individualization in the form of person-alization is 'writ large', for example in New Labour's five-year strategy (see Blair 2004b; DfES 2004):

The central characteristic of such a new system will be personalisation – so that the system fits to the individual rather than the individual having to fit the system ... and as young people begin to train for work, a system that recognises individual aptitudes and provides as many tailored paths to employment as there are people and jobs. And the corollary of this is that the system must be both freer and more diverse – with more flexibility to help meet individual needs; and more choices between courses and types of provider, so that there really are different and personalised opportunities available. (DfES 2004, p. 4)

Thus far the chapter has offered a critique of competi-tiveness and the surrounding state rhetoric. There is however another argument rooted in the way in which economic and social relations are imagined and thought to have been transformed within the competitiveness settlement. These arguments centre upon the work of writers such as Beck (1999), Castells (2000) and Giddens (2000), who argue quali-tative changes have arisen that undermine and transform class relations, changes which have also served to unpick its former collectivity. These ideas are set within a conceptual framework that rests with the risk society and the shift from simple to reflexive modernity. This in turn aligns with under-standings of post-Fordism, the third way and a model of the social formation that sits comfortably with a fluid system of networked relations. Within such a framework earlier notions of class become redundant and, in Beck's terms, become a 'Zombie' category. Beck links these processes to individualization, a feature of modernity and the breakup of traditional patterns of life. It is also a process that has deepened over the last 20 or 30 years as a result of:

- instantaneous global communication.
- the growth of neo-liberalism and the new right.
- the shift from Fordism to post-Fordism and the breakup of work-based communities.
- the fragmentation of working-class communities.
- the fragmentation of youth culture and the break away from class-based forms.
- the shift towards consumption as the basis of identity.
- the notion of *identity as a reflexive life project.*

This notion of identity emphasizes reflexivity, choice, life projects and individualization. Beck notes:

> Let us be clear what 'individualization' means. It does *not* mean individuation – how to become a unique person. It is *not* Thatcherism, not market individualism, not atomization. On the contrary individualization is a *structural* concept, related to the welfare state; it means 'institutionalized individualism'. Most of the rights and entitlements of the welfare state for example, are designed for individuals ... people are invited to constitute themselves as individuals: to plan, understand, design themselves as individuals and, should they fail, to blame themselves. (1999, p. 9)

The individual is encouraged to acquire a 'realistic' understanding of economic relations and the ways in which these impact on their life. This carries with it forms of individualization and an emphasis upon self-responsibility, which Rose has described as etho-politics:

> Etho-politics seeks to act upon conduct by acting upon the forces thought to shape the values, beliefs, moralities that themselves are

thought to determine the everyday mundane choices that human beings make as to how they lead their lives ...

If disciplinary [power] individualises and normalises, and bio-power collectivises and socialises, etho-politics concerns itself with the self techniques necessary for responsible self government and the relations between one's obligations to oneself and one's obligations to others. (1999, pp. 477–8)

Class becomes refocused and when considered is constructed in terms of cultural privilege or disadvantage, both of which are seen as amenable to technicist resolution (Brown, 2000). Whilst we can remoralize the excluded and undermine the reproduction of privilege through the imposition of merito-cratic procedures, the consequence is that structural relations become sidelined, individualization is deepened and class re-imagined as a proxy for the cultural (Ecclestone, 1999; Fryer, 1999). Against this we need to recognize the continued salience of class as a structural phenomenon and the deepening of class inequalities, not only during the Conservative governments' period of office during the 1980s and 1990s but also under Blair's New Labour governments (see for example, Gillborn and Mirza, 2000; Lauder and Brown, 2003; Lauder et al., 2004; THES, 2004). However the analyses of Beck and others, whilst recognizing the salience of these structural relations, never-theless sets these in a qualitatively different context to the recent past. Class relations are seen to be far more fluid and less tangible than was previously the case. Thus for example, in a discussion of poverty Giddens (2003, p. 21) suggests a significant number of people will experience poverty at some stage, but that the majority will move out of it within a relatively short period of time. Arguments such as these have profound policy implications. They align closely with new understandings of the social structure as well as those concerned with individualization and self-responsibilization. The consequence of arguments which stress the fluidity of social relations is that the language once used to describe educational relations is viewed as no longer appropriate and the language of class reproduction no longer seen as a suitable metaphor (see Gewirtz and Cribb, 2003). The complexity of class relations and their lack of determinacy means that whilst one can read back from educational outcomes or occupational positions to class relations, one cannot track forward from class positions to educational outcomes. This latter process is both so complex and mediated by so many variables that the attempt is rendered pointless. Thus, for example, an individual's habitus, forms of social, cultural, symbolic and economic capital all impinge upon this process, as does the lived experience of educational relations, and finally, with serendipity or happenstance similarly playing a part (Bloomer, 1997; Bloomer and Hodkinson, 2001; Lawy, 2003). Two points need to be made. First, explanations deemed determinist have more often than not sought to recognize complexity so that they can take into account the fluidity of social relations. Class is a dynamic concept, constantly being re-formed and reorganized. We could draw on Gramsci's notion of hegemony that reflects this process, one through which the dominant social bloc attempts to secure its interests. Alternatively, we could draw on Bourdieu (and Wacquant 1992), as much current writing does, to examine the relationship between the wider social context – the field of power and habitus – as well as exploring individual practice. This would in Ball's (2004, p. 7) terms allow us to examine the way in which 'class gets done'. Unsurprisingly changes in the social structure and class relations have impacted on these processes.

This loss of collectivity derives from the socio-economic context within which we are now placed. Savage (2003) in his review of Ball (2003) offers a slightly different position on these issues, arguing that class has not so much become occluded, but that middle-class notions of individualization have become hegemonic. The middle class has become the 'universal-particular class'. Such an analysis draws our attention to questions of power and ideology and the manner in which our understanding of the social formation impacts upon our analysis (see Reay, 2003). Paradoxically, such relations become less visible, and as far as class is concerned, there is not a strong sense of the way in which 'class gets done'.

[Class] is an identity based upon modes of being and becoming and forms of distinction that are realised and reproduced in specific social locations. We 'think' and are 'thought by' class. It is about being something and not being something else. It is relational. Class is also a trajectory, a path through space and time, a 'history of transactions'. We are not always the same or always able to be the same, as the world around us changes. 'Real world classes are constantly being constructed around us, people are constantly doing class' (Connell, 1983, p. 148, cited in Ball, 2004, p. 7)

Lauder and Brown (2003) draw our attention to the manner in which the neo-liberal state has attempted to reconfigure and re-form class relations. Their argument is important as it provides a contextualization for processes of individualization. Individual action planning, the personalization and allied commodification of the curriculum sit comfortably alongside these processes. This type of examination calls for a political analysis of educative processes.

Savage's analysis points towards the hegemony of middle-class interests in the construction of individualization. An awareness of the social structure as well as the patterning of social inequality, not only along the lines of class, but also those of gender and race, needs to be placed in the foreground. Patrick Ainley offers a rather different take on these questions. He suggests class structure has undergone a number of changes in recent history, resulting in three major shifts (Ainley, 2005a, b). There has been a threefold shift in the class structure away from a conventional triangular representation characterized by a small upper class at the apex and a large working-class segment at its base. At the height of the social democratic settlement the class structure was represented as having an expanding and relatively privileged middle class. Finally the current class structure is represented as one in which there is a mass 'working-middle' class that is separate from the upper class and a casualized underclass. Ainley describes this class structure as:

an Americanised class structure in which a new division within the employed population divides the respectable 'working-middle' from a new, casualised and un-, under- or worthlessly qualified, so-called 'underclass'. (Ainley, 2005a, p. 4)

The preceding has indicated that there are a number of different ways in which we can make sense of changes in the class structure. Ainley's analysis points towards the prole-tarianization of sections of the middle class who now face forms of insecurity and risk that historically confronted the working class. Although Ainley's argument is placed at some distance from that favoured by Savage, it does not necessarily sit in contradiction with the ideological representation of the middle class as the 'universal-particular' class. Indeed the formation of a mass 'working-middle' class that rests alongside processes of individualization and the pervasiveness of risk and insecurity sits easily with this apparent 'Americanization' of the class structure as it serves to occlude the collective processes involved.

The economy, social justice and individualization

This chapter has argued that the relationship between the competitive settlement and upskilling is at best overstated. The suggestion that the information knowledge society requires ever increasing levels of skills is based in part upon a misrec-ognition of changes in the class structure with that of skill. The logic of this argument is to suggest that the association between socio-economic changes and moves towards social justice is an ideological distortion. The assumption of consensus and that the needs of capital, the individual and wider society can be reconciled in a manner that serves all, is again misleading as it underplays the antagonistic relations present within society. This means that educational policies which seek to serve the interests of capital in the hope that this will result in greater social justice are doomed to fail in the long term. Capital is highly malleable and will pursue whatever route is available to maximize profitability. Currently within the UK Fordist work relations exist in tandem with neo-Fordist and, for some, post-Fordist ones. However the exact form in which these are articulated will be dependent upon the balance of force and the outcome of the struggle between capital and labour.

Educational policy, as it is currently configured, is marked by processes that centre upon the individual, with personalization and individualization being emphasized. Current policy occludes the structural and collective processes in which personalization is placed. The consequence is that the myth of meritocracy is being reconstituted in new economic and social conditions, but which, as in the past, ultimately blames the individual for educational failure.

To offset these conservative processes we need to reinstate a concern for an education that breaks free of its neo-liberal moorings and moves towards a politicized understanding of educational and economic relations. Such an education and policy context would reinstate an interest in those reproductive and collective processes that serve to generate inequality. For only by doing so will we be able to address social justice issues and be in a position to think about the way in which we can interrupt or question these. The dynamic of economic change, even if it were in the direction of upskilling, would not be sufficient to interrupt the ongoing generation of a range of inequalities embedded in capitalist relations and the dynamic of such an economy and society. There is a need to develop an educational and social politics that transcends these limitations and thereby moves towards a society characterized by the pursuit of social justice.

3
Work-based learning and social justice: 'Learning to Labour' and the new vocationalism

Here I draw upon and develop a number of arguments introduced in the previous chapter,[1] particularly those concerned with the competitive settlement and the role of education in this economic project. Work-based learning (WBL) and the creation of work-based knowledge has come to be seen as an important feature of competitiveness. By engaging in learning at the workplace employees, at whatever level, will be able to develop knowledge and skills that can be used to enhance the effectiveness of the organization in which they are employed. These types of argument rest easily with those that discuss the learning organization and lifelong learning as well as those that emanate from the state concerned with competitiveness. Within this chapter the key focus will be upon the new vocationalism that is oriented towards young people, although there will be some links made to the more general argument concerned with WBL and knowledge. The current version of the new vocationalism has much in common with that of the 1970s and 1980s, both being preoccupied with the failings of mainstream school and directed towards underachieving, disaffected young people (see Bates *et al.*, 1984).

The chapter explores work-based learning in the context of current changes taking place in vocational education and training in England. It seeks to locate these within an understanding of the economy and the way in which work-based knowledge is construed. The analysis of these issues draws upon literature that examines the work-based experiences of young people. This serves to illustrate the tension between understandings of WBL that stress knowledge creation and those oriented towards young people disaffected from schooling. Such an analysis allows an engagement with notions of social justice, providing an opportunity to address the rhetorical question, 'Learning to Labour', posed in the chapter's title. It concludes by suggesting that if work-based learning is to move beyond forms of occupational socialization there is a need to critique its underlying assumptions and seek out spaces for a progressive practice underpinned by a commitment to social justice.

Before exploring the main arguments I would like to raise a number of caveats. First, WBL has been associated with the acquisition of workplace qualifications. Boud and Symes draw a distinction between work-based knowledge/learning and learning in the workplace:

> Work-based learning needs to be distinguished from workplace learning, that form of learning that occurs on a day-to-day basis at work as employees acquire new skills or develop new approaches to solving problems. No formal educational recognition normally accrues to such learning, whether or not it is organized systematically. The emergence of work-based learning acknowledges that work, even on a day-to-day basis, is imbued with learning opportunities (Garrick, 1998), heretofore not recognized as educationally significant or worthwhile. Work-based learning gives academic recognition to these opportunities, when suitably planned and represented. (2000, p. 14)

This chapter does not examine particular types of work-based qualification, but rather seeks to explore work-based learning, placing it in a more general and cultural context, allowing questions of identity and the cultural production of subjectivity to be raised. In a similar fashion the assessment regimes present in WBL rest alongside the production and validation of preferred forms of learner identity and autonomy (Ecclestone, 2002).

Second, the movement towards WBL derives from a particular understanding of the economy and labour market

needs. This economic understanding sits alongside an interpretation of the types of knowledge and skill required for
successful performance at work. Elements of performativity
and instrumentalism can be seen in these approaches to
WBL.

> Within performative organisational cultures, *quality* is defined as
> the best equation achievable between inputs and outputs (Lyotard,
> 1997). The organisation's overriding goal is to optimise performance
> by maximising outputs (benefits) and minimising inputs (costs) and
> thereby provide 'value-for-money'. Lyotard calls this the 'principle of
> performativity'. (Elliott, 2001a, p. 193)

These arguments suggest that waged labour is the most
appropriate locale in which to develop such knowledge and
skill. There is a strong performative thrust in such arguments
which are critical of much that passes for education in
schools, universities and colleges. Such education is seen as
divorced from the real world of work. Mainstream education
is castigated for being too abstract and disciplinary bound
and thereby separated from 'real-world' concerns with 'what
works'. Although this has been the basis of a critique of
education for some years, it has gained increasing salience
as a result of the assumed move towards post-Fordist work
relations and concomitant changes in the way in which work-
based knowledge is construed.

Work-based learning

In England there is a significant concern with addressing
labour market needs, particularly at Level 3,[2] which corresponds to and includes A levels. Vocational provision at
this level is concerned with the preparation of craft and
technician labour where it is assumed there are shortages
(HM Treasury, *Skills in the Global Economy*, 2004; Leitch,
2005). Reflecting these ideas the 2006 white paper on *Further
Education* states:

A system which focuses on employability and aims to support the future success of young people and adults will be one which responds more and more sharply to the needs and demands of its customers – learners and employers ...

We propose to introduce a new entitlement to free tuition for a first full level 3 qualification for 19–25 year olds ... This will help us to tackle an area of particular weakness in skills development in this country. In many other countries, much larger numbers of young adults achieve level 2 and 3 qualifications. (DfES, 2006, p. 34)

The WBL route is seen to address this shortfall by offering young people the opportunity to develop work-based skills whilst simultaneously gaining credentials that provide the possibility of progression in education and training.

Transforming the quality and quantity of vocational learning for young people is at the heart of our 14–19 agenda. We need vocational pathways from the age of 14 which maximise young people's participation at 16, attainment by 19 and progression into higher education and skilled employment. This puts work-based learning at centre stage of Government priorities. (DfES, 2002a, p. 25)

Such a pathway seeks to attract those young people who are impatient with the academism of the school curriculum and who wish to acquire useful and practically oriented education and training experiences. These concerns have been developed and deepened in the DfES's *14–19: Opportunity and Excellence* (2003), in which there is an aspiration to increase the status of vocational education, placing it on an equal footing with the academic. This is to be achieved through the development of a unified qualification framework in which the distinction between academic and vocational forms of education would be weakened. At the time of writing this goal has been undermined as a result of the commitment to retain A levels (see DfES, 2005a). However, in 2003 the DfES's *14–19: Opportunity and Excellence* states in relation to long-term reform:

These changes will offer students greater choice, coherence and quality. They should help to improve participation and achievement while avoiding further major upheaval in a system that has undergone substantial recent change. But we believe that longer-term reform is needed. And there is a growing consensus that such change should:

- provide a much stronger vocational offer;
- allow for manageable assessment, which recognizes all of a young person's achievement;
- broaden choice and stretch students, with a unified framework of qualifications.

Such changes could improve student motivation and make applied training as important as academic learning. A unified framework would be designed to provide opportunities for young people of all abilities, by promoting progression from Foundation through Intermediate to Advanced levels. Baccalaureate-style qualifications of this kind work well abroad. We believe that this model, designed to suit English circumstances, could tackle long-standing English problems. But a new qualifications system must meet the needs of higher education and employers if it is to be introduced. (p. 7)

The Tomlinson Committee was established to examine the developments necessary to transform 14–19 learning so as to meet the aspirations of *14–19: Opportunity and Excellence* and reported in 2004. Whilst the aspiration to create a vocational pathway has stayed in place, as has the development of overarching diplomas, the radicalism of the Tomlinson Report has been undermined as a result of the retention of A levels (DfES, 2005a). The white paper *14–19 Education and Skills* calls for 'greater stretch and challenge' (DfES, 2005a, p. 63) as well as for increased differentiation at A level so that universities will be able to choose between 'the highest performing candidates' (p. 63). This elitist and exclusionary focus sits uneasily and is in something of a contradiction to New Labour's commitment to social justice (but see Allen, 2005a, b).

One group that vocational pathways seeks to address are those young people who, whilst academically able, are disengaged from the school curriculum. They are the type of respondents who featured in Unwin and Wellington's (2001) study of modern apprenticeship and who sought to combine practical work-based experience with the acquisition of qualifications. The concerns here echo those of an earlier failed intervention, *the technical and vocational initiative.* In the early 1980s this sought to introduce vocational pathways for the whole ability range in schools but was undermined by Thatcherite educational policies as well as by the tripartism that is a persistent feature of English education (Dale *et al.*, 1990; Gleeson, 1988). However at the time, as with the current interest in the development of vocational pathways, there is an interest in social justice and cohesion as well as in the provision of equal educational opportunities. This concern with social justice seeks not only to validate academic skills and knowledge but also those deriving from the workplace that are of a practical nature. This sits alongside the provision of equal educational opportunity as it seeks to validate forms of knowledge and skill previously devalued in the educational system. By so doing the interests of social cohesion are furthered. *The Learning Age* notes, 'learning contributes to social cohesion and fosters a sense of belonging, responsibility and identity' (DfEE, 1998b, p. 11). These themes are reflected in three orientations to WBL, the first of which caters for those who are academically able but disengaged from the academic curriculum. The second is oriented towards those who are disaffected from and underachieving within the education system. For this group the work-based route is thought to provide an avenue towards inclusion by offering practical and relevant experiences that articulate with their interests and allows them to develop skills and understanding of work processes. In the third avenue WBL is thought to address equal opportunities and social justice by providing academic recognition of the skills and knowledge already acquired by those in employment that would otherwise go unrecognized.

What these approaches to WBL have in common is an interest in relevant and useful knowledge, underpinned by a critique of the exclusions embodied in academicism. Such orientations are legitimated by particular understandings of the economy as well as by the type of knowledge required to enable successful performance at work. It is important to recognize that WBL is not all of a piece being accented towards different constituencies. Although WBL is underpinned by a performative conceptualization of knowledge this is emphasized in relation to managerial and professional groups, whereas amongst those who are disaffected from schooling the disciplines of wage labour are stressed. WBL allows professionals to build upon their work-based interests in the development of knowledge directly addressing workplace issues and problem solving. The knowledge, understanding and skills produced in such a context, it is claimed, will have a greater salience to work-based problem solving and be of greater use than that produced in the academy, which may itself be distorted by unwarranted disciplinary intrusions. Work-based learning and the knowledge generated will, it is suggested, make a significant contribution to the effectiveness and efficiency of the individual learner as well as their organization. This theme has been a significant current in the Australian literature on WBL which discusses professional and managerial knowledge derived from the workplace that serves to challenge academic knowledge (Garrick and Rhodes, 2000; Symes and McIntyre, 2000).

These ideas raise questions about identity, performativity and subjectivity as well as the relation of education to these processes. The DfES's *14–19: Opportunity and Excellence* as well as *14–19 Education and Skills* seeks to validate and recognize the importance of WBL for all pupils. This is important as it not only rests with a particular understanding of the economy but also with an attempt to develop within young people the dispositions and skills thought to be required by the economy – capitalist schooling. However, there is serious tension between the ideational base upon which WBL has developed and the low-waged, low-skilled characteristics of the English economy (see Chapter 2). Similarly there is a contradiction between the rhetoric of upskilling and employer reluctance to provide adequate education and training for their workforce (Coleman and Keep, 2001; Unwin and Wellington, 2001; and see Chapter 2).

Pivotal to New Labour's education strategy is a particular construction of the global economy and the relation of schooling to this. Central to this understanding, as embodied in the competitiveness settlement, is the suggestion that if the English economy is to be successful the education system must develop learners able to add value to production processes (see for example, Avis *et al.*, 1996). This chapter considers the role of WBL within this context, paying particular attention to the way in which this is addressed in the development of vocational pathways in the 14–19 curriculum – the new vocationalism. Estelle Morris, the then secretary of state for education, writes in the foreword to *14–19: Extending Opportunities, Raising Standards*:

> In the 20th century the education system was too often a one-size-fits-all structure. It neither demanded nor provided excellent standards in education for everyone. Nor did the education system adequately target the needs of the individual pupil. (DfES, 2002b, p. 3)

And in *14–19 Education and Skills* the emphasis is upon personalization and the development of programmes that meet the needs of individual learners:

> In setting out our long-term course, we send a clear signal that our intention is that the system should be fashioned around the needs of the learner and be responsive to the needs of employers. (DfES, 2005a, p. 11)

It is hoped the development of a unified qualification framework, organized through a range of diplomas located within a highly differentiated education system that retains A levels, will be able to provide the flexibility needed by individual learners to develop their full potential as well as being able to address the needs of local employers and labour markets.

> An effective 14–19 system with good links to the labour market will look different in different places. This should reflect not only the needs of the local labour market but also the differing patterns of learning institutions and traditions in each locality, and the increasingly distinctive specialisms of local schools and colleges. (DfES, 2003, p. 15)

These moves are rather more redolent of Gramsci's descriptions of Chinese complexity, or indeed of Ball's (see Bowe *et al.*, 1992) finding that a highly differentiated education system serves to entrench and reproduce class inequalities.

> Schools of the vocational type, i.e. those designed to satisfy immediate practical interests, are beginning to predominate over the formative school, which is not immediately 'interested'. The most paradoxical aspect of it all is that this new type of school appears and is advocated as being democratic, while in fact it is destined not merely to perpetuate social differences but to crystallise them in Chinese complexities. (Gramsci, 1971, p. 40)

The development of a re-engineered 14–19 sector containing vocational pathways that are flexible and responsive to the needs of individuals and employers will, it is claimed, also meet the requirements of the economy, society and individual.

> In the 21st century, to be prosperous, the economy will depend heavily on the creativity and skills of its people. In a knowledge economy it is vital that we tap the potential of every one of our citizens. (DfES, 2002b, p. 3)

Such arguments are premised upon a particular and rhetorical understanding of the English economy, its potential for development as well as those factors that inhibit this. It is also underpinned by particular understandings of the way in which educational provision should respond to these economic imperatives as well as by a particular understanding of social justice which sees the needs of the economy, society and individual as being in alignment. New Labour's construction of social justice ties it to notions of rights and responsibilities that make it incumbent upon the individual to avail themselves of the educational and training opportunities provided by the state. Giddens (2002) discusses the shift from the redistributive state to the social investment state. In this case social justice is not concerned with an egalitarian redistribution of income or wealth, rather the state seeks to interrupt the reproduction of disadvantage by providing opportunities for the individual to better themselves. Giddens' approach rests within a redistributive logic that focuses upon opportunity rather than income and wealth. For Giddens (2002) there is a trade-off between redistributive justice in relation to income and wealth and a meritocracy that underpins economic and social regeneration (see Gewirtz, 2002, for a discussion of New Labour redistributive justice).

Within the competitiveness settlement the worker is seen as the key factor of production with economic success deriving from the application of value-added waged labour. This process sits alongside a particular and related understanding of knowledge, one stripped of universal pretensions. Knowledge becomes tied to the enactment of skill in the workplace. It is at this juncture that WBL becomes important. By learning in the workplace the worker can contribute to the organization's knowledge base, thereby adding value. This type of knowledge production will be localized in the sense that it will address the concerns of a particular institution seeking to render that organization more efficient. The type of knowledge developed will be based upon organizational interests and requirements and will therefore tend to preclude the development of critical insights.

Low-skilled and low-waged work remains a reality for large numbers of the working population. These wage relations encourage market competition on price rather than quality, which in the case of the latter would serve to develop the skills of the workforce. In addition the policy rhetoric ignores, or at least plays down, the different routes that can be pursued to gain competitive advantage. These processes are compounded by New Labour's interest in sustaining flexible labour markets and seeing waged labour as the route to social inclusion. Such a strategy, despite minimum wage legislation, serves to sustain a low-waged economy. The significance of these issues in a discussion of work-based learning is to locate this within its socio-economic context. It also raises questions about the generality of WBL and its relationship to an economy characterized by low-skilled and low-waged work. If WBL is to seriously address issues of social inclusion and cohesion, it would need to be placed within a framework that seeks to challenge the forms of working relations characteristic of much of the English economy. To do otherwise would locate WBL within the reproduction of existing social and cultural relations. It would operate on a terrain described by Cathcart and Esland (1985) that seeks to produce compliant-creative workers who are complicit in their own exploitation:

> The expectation is that workers will be creative in the furthering of capitalist goals but compliant towards the social relations and structures they find in the workplace. (Cathcart and Esland, 1985, p. 185)

To interrupt such processes would require rethinking WBL so that it could move beyond its alignment with employer interests.

Boud and Symes' description of WBL and workplace learning was commented upon earlier, they noted:

> The emergence of work-based learning acknowledges that work, even on a day-to-day basis, is imbued with learning opportunities (Garrick, 1998), heretofore not recognized as educationally significant or worthwhile. Work-based learning gives academic recognition to these opportunities, when suitably planned and represented. (2000, p. 14)

The task is not simply recognizing the potentiality of WBL for employees but to return to older concerns that sought to use work educatively to examine the labour process and surrounding social relations (Finn, 1987; Moore, 1983). Such a project is in part challenged by the way workplace knowledge is construed within 'reflexive modernity'. These constructions build upon the long-standing realization that variable labour creates surplus value and the pursuit of continuous improvement rests within such an understanding. However, 'postmodern' conceptualizations of knowledge reflect a qualitative shift in the way in which knowledge is understood. The particular and localized nature of workplace knowledge is stressed, as is its lack of universality and the way in which it seeks to address organizational needs to improve effectiveness. Such conceptualizations imply that not all work has the potential for knowledge creation and therefore WBL (Fuller and Unwin, 2003). The focus here is upon learning as well as knowledge creation that makes a contribution towards organizational effectiveness. These can be set against older concerns that sought to use work educatively (Moore, 1983; and see Shilling, 1988). If we were to return to those key groups for whom it is thought WBL is appropriate (professionals, craft workers, practically and vocationally oriented young people, disaffected pupils) the first three have the potential for creative engagement. Whereas for the final group, disaffected pupils, WBL is rather more concerned with compliance and inculcation into the disciplines of the workplace.

Knowledge

A thriving knowledge society must be cosmopolitan and open; it must reward talent and creativity; it must invest in people and education. The radical innovation and knowledge creation that underpins modern economic growth thrives in cultures that are democratic and dissenting; that are open to new ideas from unusual sources; in which authority and élites are constantly questioned and challenged. (Leadbeater, 1999, p. ix)

The move towards work-based learning adopts a particular construction of knowledge and the economy that sits comfortably with the competitiveness settlement (see for example, Garrick and Rhodes, 2000; Symes and McIntyre, 2000a). This view of knowledge draws on a number of the elements found in the critique of modernity and aligns with the suggestion that social formations have moved away from simple modernity towards reflexive modernization. Such a movement carries a shift from mode 1 disciplinary-based knowledge to mode 2, which is characterized by interdisciplinarity:

... a transformation of knowledge, a move away from ... Mode 1 knowledge which is homogeneous, rooted in strong disciplines which are hierarchical, and transmitted to novitiates in an apprentice–master relationship, to Mode 2 knowledges which are non-hierarchical, pluralistic, transdisciplinary, fast changing, and socially responsive to a diversity of needs such as students' dispositions and industrial priorities. (Smith and Webster, 1997, p. 104)

Chappell *et al.* suggest that the new epistemological discourses,

... appear to unsettle modern understandings of knowledge by reversing the traditional binaries that privilege one form of knowledge construction over its 'other'. Today, epistemological discourses emphasize knowledge constructed as practical, interdisciplinary, informal, applied and contextual over knowledge constructed as theoretical, disciplinary, formal, foundational and generalizable. (2000, p. 137)

The movement towards mode 2 knowledge articulates with post-Fordist understandings of work relations as well as the claim that valid knowledge can be gained at work, which in turn can be used to enhance organizational performance and effectiveness. These arguments have an affinity with the suggestion that value-added waged labour is the key to competitiveness and that high-skilled, high-trust, high-waged working relations will create the conditions in which continuous improvement can take place. Such a context requires that tacit and informal workplace knowledge becomes formalized, and that such knowledge is generalizable across a particular organization so as to enhance performance. Work-based learning can be seen as part of this process in as much as it leads to the formalization of that which was hidden, transmogrifying it into generalizable, though institutionally specific, forms of knowledge.

What discussions of reflexive modernity add to the debate is the claim that academic and disciplinary-based knowledge, rooted in the academy, is out of kilter with these new conditions. Disciplinary-based knowledge, with its hierarchical and hidebound structures, cannot respond quickly enough to changing organizational needs. This knowledge is also seen as elitist and exclusionary when contrasted with work-based knowledge that arises through an engagement with work practices. The current attempt to validate vocational and practical knowledge in schools can be seen as part of this process (DfES, 2003). In the case of work-based knowledge it is thought of as being democratized and rid of its elitist pretensions (see the discussion in Garrick and Rhodes, 2000). Knowledge derived at the workplace is thus thought to be more authentic and useful than that derived in the academy as it has the potential to enhance individual and institutional performance. This ideational framework forms a regime of truth and system of governability in which the worker/learner must constantly reflect upon the labour process with a view to continual improvement (Edwards and Usher, 2000; Scheeres and Solomon, 2000). This is the context of performativity in which there is an affinity between the way in which knowledge is construed and work processes. However, the reality of work relations is very far from these constructions, which nevertheless are attempting to form preferred under-standings of work. The preceding conceptualizations provide ideological supports for instrumental and pragmatic forms of knowledge concerned with 'what works' (Barnett, 2000). Similarly, they operate with an idealization of work relations that is seen as being free from social relations, thereby normal-izing and validating workplace relations. Any recognition of social antagonism or patterns of exploitation arising at the site of waged labour are thereby marginalized. Paradoxically such interpretation of knowledge and its relation to work seeks to construct the worker/learner, both atomistically and collectively, as capital. Beckett cites Handy's comments on intellectual capital to illustrate this process:

> But, in the age of intellectual capital, who owns the capital? It is not the shareholders. It can't be in any real sense. The people who own the capital are the core workers of the company. In other words it's the assets who own the assets. (2000, p. 75)

From a slightly different stance Rikowski, commenting on 'human capital', writes:

There is force-expenditure (of human labour-power), but also development of this labour-power on the basis of capital, labour-power capitalised – and as labour-power is inseparable from the person, then we have personhood capitalised, humans capitalised, human capital. Capital becomes a living social force within the human and internal and internalised social relation within individuals – and this is the basis of the transhuman; it is this which makes us 'extra-human'. Capital is not just 'out there'; we are it, it is us. (1999, pp. 70–1)

The interest in developing work-based knowledge to enhance efficiency reflects a recognition of the way in which variable labour power produces surplus value. As such the interest in work-based knowledge is not new, but what is, is the increasing significance being placed upon such knowledge in winning competitive advantage. It should be noted that workplace knowledge has always been 'owned' by the worker, the trick has been for capital to appropriate this and use it for its own interests. Rikowski draws our attention to the equivocations and contradictions of this process in which the worker becomes 'human capital', in that they embody the contradictions surrounding this process and thus are an embodiment of class struggle. However these processes operate in a number of different ways. In some cases, as with routinized forms of labour, the worker may become aware of ways in which a particular task could be performed more efficiently. Calls for continuous improvement may encourage workers to share this knowledge so that it can be incorporated into the labour process (see Avis, 1996b; Garrahan and Stewart, 1992). In other instances where work is less routinized the forms of knowledge generated will be akin to mode 2 and will have more to do with the creativity of those involved. But in both cases social relations ensure the creativity of the worker is framed by an acceptance of capitalist relations.

There is tension between a new regime of truth oriented towards the appropriation of the creativity and knowledge-producing potential of the workforce and an older regime that construed work-based learning as a means of habituating disaffected young people to the disciplines of the workplace (Finn, 1987; Hollands, 1990). However, what is important in current conditions is the urgency with which capital seeks to appropriate all types of knowledge to contribute to the generation of surplus value.

Vocational pathways – learner dispositions

The development of vocational pathways at 14+ addresses at one level some young people's disaffection from schooling yet simultaneously seeks to encourage progression to higher levels (see DfES, 2002a, b). However, at the same time, as is the case with curriculum 2000, these pathways work within the academic/vocational divide. *Schools Achieving Success* states:

> For the first time there will also be the opportunity of a predominantly vocational programme for those with the aptitude, beginning at 14 and going right through to degree level. Such a programme might include a significant element of work related learning from 14, followed by a Modern Apprenticeship or full time vocational study at college and then a Foundation Degree for those who have the potential. (DfES, 2001, p. 31)

Such differentiation within institutions will be matched by a similar process in schools and colleges. In addition the development of foundation and advanced apprenticeships will introduce differentiation into the post-16 youth training system with consequences for progression. However all these interventions seek to enhance and incorporate work-based learning. This can be seen in New Labour's development of Centres of Vocational Excellence in Further Education (COVE).

> Centres of Vocational Excellence will develop new, and enhance existing, excellent vocational provision which is focused on meeting the skills needs of employers, nationally, sectorally, regionally and locally. They will seek to give a greater number of individuals from all

backgrounds access to the high quality vocational training which they need to succeed in a modern economy. (LSC, 2001, p. 3)

COVE will also reach back into the compulsory sector with a view to enhancing the vocational education of 14–19-year-olds – WBL is pivotal to this strategy. Learners will increasingly find themselves confronting a highly differentiated education system through which they will have to steer a path. At the time of writing it seems unlikely that a unified qualification framework will be developed in the immediate future that attempts to break down the division between the academic and vocational, other than the minor changes proposed in the white paper *14–19 Education and Skills* (see DfES, 2003, 2005a, 2006). However, whatever the outcome, these developments will take place within an education system that seeks to promote flexibility and differentiation. Such a system will, it is claimed, be cognizant of local labour market needs, the needs of learners and the varied institutional arrangements for educational provision – the ensuing complexity will be enormous. Learners will confront a plethora of institutional provision marked by various forms of specialization running throughout the education system and culminating in an increasingly differentiated higher education sector (Reay *et al.*, 2005).

Vocational pathways will be developed for those who have become disaffected from school, and may also become an option for those who have an interest in the practical development of skill at the workplace, whilst at the same time gaining qualifications for higher education. Such pathways, as found in modern apprenticeships, will sit alongside other academic and vocational provision. Such differentiation may be compounded by the development of specialist secondary schools, colleges and so on (DfES 2006). An increasingly fragmented and specialized education system marked by a plethora of pathways may find itself serving to reproduce the patterns of inequality and structural differentiation present in wider society. Jamieson (1993), citing Boudon, writes approvingly:

> As Boudon (1974) observed, in societies structured by class and other inequalities, the greater the variety of different routes through the education system, the greater the likelihood that the system will reproduce the existing pattern of differentiation. (1993, p. 215)

This may arise in a number of ways. The differential costs involved in participating in the education system serve to reproduce class inequalities – consider the current debate over top-up university fees in England (see ongoing debates in THES, 2002–6). Neo-liberal policies that emphasize choice are likely to reproduce class inequalities as they draw upon familial, social and financial resources (for a discussion see Bowe *et al.*, 1992). Relatedly, findings from the sociology of education suggest those who possess cultural capital will make best use of a differentiated education system to secure class advantage (Bourdieu, 2002; Gewirtz, 2002; Wolf, 2002).

Early studies addressing the transition to work and youth training experiences illustrate the way in which these lead to the formation and production of identities that reproduce class relations (Avis, 1984, 1991b; Bates, 1991; Finn, 1987; Hollands, 1990; Moos, 1979; and see Mizen, 1995). Moos, for example, illustrated the way in which the early youth training schemes sought to prepare young people for casualized and intermittent waged labour. Key to these processes were particular orientations to mental and manual labour. Many of the early studies focused on underachieving youth and explored resistance to schooling that served to propel young people towards waged labour. These studies suggested schooling had marginal relevance to the lives or interests of these young people and mental labour was thought to be overly abstract and separate from real-world concerns. Willis's (1977) work, for example, illustrated the way in which young people associated mental labour with effeminacy, and Stafford's (1991) work exploring experience on a youth training scheme demonstrated the way in which trainees actively resisted practices that were reminiscent of the classroom. These studies showed the way in which mental/manual divisions were associated with the development of class and gendered identities that articulated with reproductive processes. Such processes are not necessarily all of a piece, being fractured in a variety of ways. Brown's (1987) work on 'ordinary kids' explored another aspect of these processes whereby young people minimally accepted school relations as a necessary part of the route to respectable working-class jobs. Whilst this work may appear dated it does raise questions about formative processes and the reproduction of class-based identities, themes bypassed in current writing about work-based learning. Central to the formation of class-based identities is the orientation towards schooling as well as to mental/manual divisions, with the latter associated with practical work-based knowledge and skills. Paradoxically, these orientations remain in place although they have been reworked within current conditions.

The majority of young people now remain in education and training post-16, with early school leaving becoming a rarity (see Wolf, 2002). In the current conditions we can see the way in which mental/manual divisions have been reworked to align with the new context in which young people find themselves. The concern with relevance remains, as does the dissatisfaction with abstract and overly academic forms of knowledge. In Ecclestone's work on GNVQs, many students were reluctant to engage with broader academic and political debate, being concerned with the more immediate and local context of practice:

> Students' responses here appear to resonate with young people's resistance to 'irrelevant' education in other studies. These GNVQ related effects presented difficulties for teachers committed to broad pastoral interpretations of personal autonomy or to critical autonomy. Strong views about 'relevance' and 'usefulness', combined with aversion to difficult subjects, meant that the relevance of evaluating a health campaign was easier to sell to students, for example, than evaluating competing theories in social policy. (2002, p. 154)

A similarly strong sense of the relevant was also present in Unwin and Wellington's (2001) study. The celebration of relevant practical work-based knowledge articulates with the mental/manual divide, serving to devalue and marginalize the academic against the immediacy of practice. The shift from simple to reflexive modernity serves to raise questions about the salience and validity of disciplinary and academic forms of knowledge. The concern with practice, with 'what works', with the relatively short term, and an immediate interest in practice serves to marginalize and write off disciplinary knowledge. Not only is such knowledge of passing relevance to practice, its legitimacy has become questioned in conditions of reflexive modernity.

The paradox is that the type of mode 2 knowledge that has gained legitimacy in current postmodern conditions is deeply conservative. Mode 2 knowledge articulates with a concern with 'what works'. For those involved in workplace learning the hegemony of such an epistemological framework is that knowledge can easily go no further than practice. It becomes tied to the immediacy of practice and with 'what works'. It thereby connives not only in its own construction, as a social technology, but also in the development of work-based identities that themselves are tied to a performative logic. Erased from this is an earlier concern with using work educatively, for learners to explore the nature of society and the role of waged labour within it (Moore, 1983). Instead, work-based learning becomes tied to performativity, quality systems and so on, all of which seek to uncover tacit and informal knowledge in order to enhance efficiency (Garrick and Clegg, 2000).

Work-based learning – questions and difficulties

The interest in work-based learning and the development of vocational pathways for young people is underpinned by a number of discourses. In part, work-based learning seeks to reintegrate those who are disillusioned with or disaffected from schooling by drawing on an interest in work – this is a significant element in proposed interventions for 14–19 education in England (DfES, 2002a, b, 2003, 2005a, b). It is intended through these new pathways that disaffected youth will be reintegrated into society, their talents and potential will not be wasted and they will not be excluded from progression in the education training system. In this way goals of social justice and inclusion will be met. However, as with foundation and advanced apprenticeships, there is a real question about whether employers will be able to deliver the quality of training required. This was consistently the case with earlier youth training schemes and has been a feature of modern apprenticeships, where the quality of training has been extremely variable, and sometimes exceptionally poor (Hyland, 2002; Unwin and Wellington, 2001; Wolf, 2002).

Additionally, work-based learning seeks to address the interests of those who, whilst academically able, feel out of kilter with schooling and are seeking practical experience alongside the acquisition of qualifications that offer the possibility of progression to higher education. The unevenness of the education and training experiences of this group has already been noted. The following section comments on the dominant theoretical frameworks that seek to justify and validate the move towards as well as the importance of work-based learning. Underpinning such work is the suggestion that practice and learning are conjoined, that we develop understanding through practice. This work also rests with a particular view of knowledge, suggesting that it derives from the immediacy of practice and is therefore situated within a particular context. This suggests that if 'real' learning is to take place it should be acquired in the context where the resulting knowledge can be practically applied. In other words there is a dialectic between practice, context and the production of knowledge. Brown *et al.* (1989) discuss situated cognition/ learning and claim that schooling is an inappropriate location to develop work-based practice, as the logic of schooling is different to that of occupational practice. In order to become a practitioner the learner needs to be incorporated into the rules of practice. These notions are reflected in discussions that address communities of practice and utilize the notion of core and peripheral participation. This argument suggests novitiates, through engagement in work-based practice, move from the periphery of a community of practice towards its core, during which time the novitiate becomes a full member (Lave and Wenger, 1991). It is recognized that this movement is not necessarily one-way, as the newcomer may have certain skills and knowledge that established practitioners lack, and consequently, at times, their positions will be reversed. However, the logic of the movement remains in place. Whilst within models of situated learning and communities of practice there are gestures towards dialogic understandings and the impact and resolutions of contradictions, these are nevertheless located within a consensual framework (see Avis *et al.*, 2002; Avis, 2005). The novitiate is being introduced to a specific community of practice through which they are being encultured into the outlook of that particular occupational group. A similar process can be seen at work in activity theory, where contradictions play a pivotal part in the resolution of difficulties as well as learning (see Engeström, 2001). However, lying behind the resolution of contradiction is a consensual framework in which it is assumed participants in the activity system share a common understanding of the goals pursued. For Engeström (2001), learning arises when contradictions are resolved (and see Young, 2001). However, such contradictions are located within a work-based context that assumes they can be consensually resolved and so paradoxically rests within the terrain of the compliant-creative worker.

It may seem that the discussion above is one step removed from the interest in work-based learning and its implications for social justice. On one level work-based learning is inclusive as it attempts to engage those disaffected from learning. However, the context in which it takes place is contradictory, and whilst it may develop young people's understanding of work, particularly with respect to knowledge and the development of located skills, this is truncated. As can be seen in the discussion of communities of practice and situated learning much of this learning is individualized, with the young person being socialized or encultured into a specific community of practice. Although there may be aspects concerned with collective problem solving and the development of collective intelligence (Brown and Lauder, 2000), this takes place on a very particular terrain, one that fails to address antagonism at the site of waged labour. This partly derives from the basis upon which work-based knowledge develops, but is also a consequence of arguments about reflexive modernization that suggest Marxist explanations of work processes developed during simple modernity are no longer appropriate.

Within the 14–19 context WBL seeks to validate the vocational as well as young people's interest in the practical aspects of work. As such it seeks to value and recognize these interests and potential skills in young people – skills and interests that have traditionally been devalued when set against the academic. There is an implication for social justice in that these processes could be interpreted as a politics of recognition, an attempt to value the interests and concerns of young people who have been marginalized by the education system. Such an argument has salience in the current period when academic and disciplinary-based knowledge is increasingly challenged for its lack of applicability and arbitrariness (Bourdieu, 2002). Adopting an alternative position Michael Young seeks to reclaim the objectivity of academic knowledge by calling for a social realist approach, one that recognizes the social processes involved, but that acknowledges:

> the context-independent characteristics of knowledge and that the powerful discontinuities between knowledge and common sense ... [are] the real conditions that enable us to gain knowledge about the world. (2003, pp. 113, 114).

Work-based knowledge and the interest in the vocational is tied to a performative logic that seeks to address the needs of capital. Young people's interest in the vocational and practical, in the immediacy of experience, in the 'real' world of work should neither be discounted nor devalued. At the same time they should have access to other forms of knowledge that offer a critique of the performative logic of WBL in order to avoid habituation to the disciplines of the workplace. It is here that insights derived from academic and disciplinary forms of knowledge have a part to play. Young reminds us that such a curriculum:

> ... is always partly designed to enable students to acquire concepts and forms of understanding and learn how to apply them in different contexts, it is also always organized to preserve vested interests and maintain the status quo. (1998a, p. 5 and see Nash, 1999).

Whilst WBL may be criticized for being placed within a performative logic, it will always be more than just that. This is because learners at the workplace may experience some of the contradictions and tensions surrounding waged labour. The work experience of Shilling's (1988) young people served to dissuade at least some from entering factory work (and see JVET, 2003). In the same way learners could use work-based experience to engage with and critique the academic and disciplinary-based curriculum. There is the potential for dialogue across these domains, with learners having a right to access these differing forms of knowledge. Such a stance would bring together a politics of recognition and that of distribution, in the sense that whilst the practical and vocational is valued learners are also provided with access to other forms of knowledge.

Conclusion – social justice

This chapter has explored the policy context within which WBL is placed, has touched upon young people's experiences and has explored current debates in this area. The English economy is marked by skill polarization, having a large low-skilled and semi-skilled and a small high-skilled sector. Policy rhetoric focuses upon the needs of the economy for skilled and creative workers and this is the thrust that lies behind calls for the reinvigoration of vocational education. However, it is likely that those involved in vocational programmes will encounter the contradictions of policy – the inability of the economy to provide appropriate work. Nevertheless

WBL sits comfortably with the competitiveness settlement in which the key to competitive advantage lies in value-added waged labour. The worker, either individually or as part of a collective process, is seen as fundamental to economic success. The stress placed upon WBL sits comfortably with the formation of class relations as well as with the development of forms of subjectivity required by the economy. The worker/learner is encouraged to render explicit their tacit and informal work knowledge and to contribute towards processes of continuous improvement. To the extent that these are successful the young person will have 'learned to labour', with WBL producing dispositions that connive with performative interests. This process articulates with an interest in narrowly defined notions of relevance and practice. However, there are a number of contradictions surrounding this, not least the ambivalence of employers to education and training, as well as a significant tension between the exploitation of workers to create surplus value and the rhetoric of social justice. In the current period notions of work-based learning are deeply ambivalent. The critique of modernity suggests that issues of social justice and the role of education in the formation of class and other inequalities are infinitely complex. As a result WBL is seen simultaneously to face in a number of different directions. This recognition of complexity can be disabling in that its refusal to countenance dichotomies has led to the deep structures of employment relations being either ignored or minimized. If WBL is to move beyond forms of occupational socialization there is a need to critique its underpinning notions and challenge the reproduction of communities of practice. It needs to recover Dewey's concern with using young people's interest in work as a vehicle through which to explore the economic and social structures of society (see Hager, 2000; Moore, 1983). Such a practice would be dependent upon WBL being aligned to a pedagogy that was able to move beyond the workplace, connecting social relations of work to those of the wider society. The opening up of this pedagogic space is not easy. However, those learners currently dissuaded from such questions, but who are concerned with the immediacy of practice, would have access to alternative understandings that problematize existing social relations. It is here that the critical potential of WBL resides. Without such an orientation WBL will be no more than 'learning to labour' and will fail to engage with issues of social justice in a serious fashion. A better starting point would be a 14–19 curriculum that integrated the vocational with the academic (see for example, Young, 1993, 1998a, b), rather than the development of pathways that serve to cement class differentiation. Current policy developments are at one remove from a unified curriculum, preferring instead to discuss a unified qualification framework that appears to be infinitely flexible and seeks to reflect learner need and labour market conditions as well as variations in educational provision. The very complexity of these developments is likely to lead to processes of class reproduction. Nevertheless current policies seek to open up progression routes to higher education as well as enabling movement from vocational to academic. These policy tensions create spaces in which it is possible to move beyond an instrumentalism committed to narrow work-based learning and training. Here lies the struggle for work-based educators committed to a critical education to wrest progressive practice from those seeking conformity in the youth of today to capitalist needs.

Notes

1 An earlier version of this chapter was presented to the British Educational Research Association Annual Conference at the University of Exeter, 12–14 September 2002 and has been published in *Journal of Education and Work*, vol. 17, no. 2, pp. 197–217.
2 Qualification by level
    Level 1:   GCSEs, O levels or equivalent at grades D–G; National Vocational Qualification (NVQ) Level 1; Business Training and Education Council (BTEC) first or general certificate; General National Vocational Qualification (GNVQ) foundation

level; Royal Society of Arts (RSA); and SCOTVEC modules

Level 2: Five or more GCSEs, O levels or equivalent grades A*–C; NVQ Level 2; BTEC first or general diploma; GNVQ intermediate level; City and Guilds Craft; RSA diploma; and BTEC, SCOTVEC first or general diploma

Level 3: Two or more A levels or equivalent; NVQ Level 3; BTEC National; Ordinary National Diploma (OND); City and Guilds Advanced Craft; and 3 or more Scottish highers

Level 4: First or other degree; NVQ Level 4; Higher National Diploma (HND); Higher National Certificate (HNC); and higher education diploma; nursing; teaching (including further education, secondary, primary and others)

Level 5: Higher degree; Doctor of Philosophy (PhD); and NVQ Level 5

These levels can be further classified into low skills (no qualification and Level 1); intermediate skills (Levels 2 and 3) and high skill (Level 4 and above).

Source: Leitch Review of Skills 2005, p. 38.

4
Learner dispositions: continuity and change

The first part of this chapter focuses upon the lived experiences of learners within further education. It seeks to explore the empirical continuities and discontinuities of learners' dispositions to post-compulsory education, as mediated through lived experience. This exploration is accompanied by an examination of the way in which theorists have attempted to understand and explain learner responses and dispositions towards these educative experiences. The chapter analyses the different ways in which learner experiences have been theorized and seeks to draw out the limits and possibilities surrounding these for the development of progressive practice. This analysis is in turn related to the way in which the socio-economic context has been understood. There is a loose affinity between shifts in theorizations of learner experience and that of the socio-economic context – both sets of theorizations in some sense play off one another. In conclusion the chapter seeks to draw out the relationship of learners' lived experience and their engendered dispositions to social justice and explores the limits and possibilities surrounding the development of progressive practice.

After a brief discussion of the early work of Venables (1967, 1974) I move on to examine analyses that drew on Marxist understandings of the reproduction of class relations, albeit that these were articulated in relation to gender and race. The analysis ends with current theorizations that emphasize the importance of learning cultures, their ongoing transformation and the relationship of these to learner identity. This part of the chapter draws upon writers associated with the ESRC (Economic and Social Research Council) *Transforming Learning Cultures project,*[1] a research programme that is one of the best-funded and certainly the most important study of learning and teaching within the sector. However, before engaging with this discussion it is important to refer back to the earlier analysis of the socio-economic context as this serves to frame the ensuing argument.

Context

The immediate post-war period has frequently been taken as the starting point for analyses of education in general and post-compulsory education and training in particular. This specific conjunctural moment has formed the benchmark against which changes in the socio-economic context, as well as the lived experience of educative relations, are made sense of. There are two types of political and academic forgetfulness that flow from this. The first is that class cultures of the time are construed as being relatively static, being marked by particular structures of masculinity and femininity. Class as a structural phenomenon is seen as being fixed and marked by genera-tional continuities. Whilst there are elements of continuity these have served to marginalize and underplay the ongoing transformation of class relations. The continuous remaking of class and alongside this the re-formation of gendered and ethnic relations together with constructions of 'whiteness' are all intertwined with class formation (Preston, 2003).

The pre-war period, marked by dislocation, brought about by economic crises impacted upon class relations. The years of the Second World War influenced class and gender relations in any number of ways and provided the ideological and material ground upon which the social democratic settlement could be built. The immediate post-war period was characterized by the development of the Keynesian welfare state as well as by the formation of the social democratic educational settlement, both of which brought and anticipated changes in class relations. The significance of the preceding is that it suggests that throughout the post-war period any moment of apparent stability needs to be understood in relation to the ongoing remaking of class relations. This means that we need to recognize and explore the complex articulation of class to the economic structure as well as its relation to education. Such processes need to be framed by an understanding of the historical genesis of class formation and the manner in which this articulated to gender and ethnicity. The second form of forgetfulness refers to the construction of the post-war period itself, in which the apparent stability and affluence of the early years were construed unproblematically as a result of the application of Keynesian economics. Yet the economy was more uneven than this picture presents, with significant inequalities present. Writers such as Abel-Smith and Townsend (1965), Coates and Silburn (1970) and many others uncovered the continuing existence and persistence of poverty within Britain at that time.

Another point to be made is that reproductive processes have always impacted against what Richard Johnson (1979a, p. 58) referred to as 'obdurately resistant material'. That is to say reproductive processes in relation to class are uneven, fractured and complex, being marked by various kinds of struggle and articulated in particular ways to structures of gender and race, and indeed those of sexuality and age. The current preoccupation with complexity is in this sense neither new nor particularly insightful, but does ask us to consider the way in which current educational and class experiences relate to the socio-economic structure, the ongoing formation of inequality and the manner in which this articulates to race and gender.

There is a large body of literature about young people's experience in further education. This work has to be set within the context of the patterning of educational inequality within the school system and the manner in which these inequalities are carried into further education. These inequalities are reflected in forms of participation, course taken, curriculum followed and modes of attendance. Young people's engagement in the sector is indicative of the play of educational inequalities and reflects the patterning of these in relation to class, race and gender. Statistical data illustrates a number of these features:

- Participation rates by 16-year-olds in post compulsory education varies by socio-economic status ... Young people aged 16 in England and Wales whose parents were in higher professional occupations in 2004 were more likely to be in full time education than young people whose parents were in routine occupations (85 per cent and 57 per cent respectively). (*Social Trends*, 2006, p. 39)
- [In 2004 there was] variation by socio-economic status in the qualifications 16 year olds in full-time education studied. This was particularly the case for those studying for GCE A level or equivalent – 74 per cent of 16 year olds whose parents were in higher professional occupations were studying for this level of qualification compared with 31 per cent of 16 year olds whose parents were in routine occupations. (*Social Trends*, 2006, p. 39)
- In England and Wales 76 per cent of pupils whose parents were in higher professional occupations achieved higher grade GCSE [A*–C] (or equivalent) in 2004, compared with 33 per cent of those in routine occupations. (*Social Trends*, 2006, p. 41)
- [Women] outperform men in vocational qualifications – 29 per cent of young women in schools and colleges gained a distinction for their advanced General National Vocational qualification in 2001/2 compared with 17 per cent of young men. (National Statistics Online, 2006a, unnumbered)
- Business was the most popular subject for both men and women taking an advanced GNVQ, the next most popular subjects differed between the sexes. Twenty five per cent of women took Health and Social Care compared with 1 per cent of men, whereas 22 per cent of men took Information Technology compared with 4 per cent of women. (National Statistics Online, 2006a, unnumbered)

- The lowest levels of GCSE attainment [2004] were among Black Caribbean pupils, particularly boys. Only 27 per cent of Black Caribbean boys and 44 per cent of girls achieved five or more A*–C grade GCSE. Pupils from Black African, other Black and mixed White and Black Caribbean groups had the next lowest levels of attainment. (National Statistics Online, 2006b, unnumbered)

Learners within further education, post-compulsory education and the learning and skills sector are diverse, being marked by divisions in relation to age, class, gender and ethnicity as well as the manner in which they participate in the sector, be it full or part time. Learners are also differentiated by the nature of the curriculum they encounter, which could move from the pre-vocational through to the academic and can be set at different levels ranging from basic skills through to degree level work.[2] The Foster review of further education (2005, p. 21) noted:

- 56% of 17 year olds in full time education in GFECs [general further education colleges] come from the bottom 3 socio-economic groups compared to 31% in sixth form colleges and 22% in maintained school sixth forms.
- 29% of learners in GFECs are from relatively disadvantaged postcode areas compared to 25% in the population as a whole.
- 14% of FE learners are from non-white ethnic groups compared to 8% in the overall population.
- 8.2% of learners in GFECs and 6.2% in sixth form colleges have a declared disability or learning difficulty.

The relationship of learners to the curriculum is complex, mediated by their experiences within the sector. In addition these educative relationships cannot be separated from the cultural baggage learners carry with them into the sector – their placement within the education system that in turn is related to the wider socio-economic and cultural conditions in which they are located. It is not possible to designate a straightforward characterization of learner experience within the sector, given that it is so diverse and indeed particular students' experience will be framed by the specificities of their engagement. The following section needs to be read with the preceding in mind, serving as a caveat for the following empirical descriptions that seek to draw together some of the findings addressing the lived experience of students in the sector.

Early work

The early work of Venables (1967, 1974) conducted in the 1960s and early 1970s was rooted within a psychological paradigm and sought to explore the experience of apprentices. Her psychological orientation led her to consider the relationship between personality and educational success. She argued that this was related to factors such as: a personality that veered towards anxiety and introversion; being the first or only child in a family; having a muscular physique; and so on (Venables, 1967, p. 158). This work not only resonated with the old sociology of education, which operated with a deficit model and examined the educability of the working class (Douglas, 1967; Halsey *et al.*, 1961) but also has a resonance with recent work which has attempted to examine the characteristics of young people and their orientations towards learning. Current state interventions have veered in this direction. New Labour's *The Learning Age: A New Renaissance for Britain* (DfEE 1998b) called for the transformation of working-class cultures to ensure that these would validate learning and thereby prepare young people for their place within the knowledge economy, as well as for lifelong learning. The Social Exclusion Unit, in *Bridging the Gap*, sought to list the characteristics of young people that precluded them from learning, stating:

the risk of non-participation [learning or work] is higher for young people if:
• Their parents are poor or unemployed
• They are members of certain minority ethnic groups

- They are in particular circumstances which create barriers to participation
  i. They are carers
  ii. They are teenage parents
  iii. They are homeless
  iv. They are or have been in care
  v. They have a learning difficulty
  vi. They have a disability
  vii. They have a mental illness
  viii. They misuse drugs or alcohol
  ix. They are involved in offending (Social Exclusion Unit, 1999, p. 48)

In the 1970s the onset of mass unemployment, particularly for young people, moved interest away from the psychological analyses of writers such as Venables towards structural analyses rooted in reproduction and resistance theories. These approaches sought to understand the role of FE in reproducing the social and sexual division of labour. Amongst others, Gleeson and Mardle (1980), Avis (1984, 1985), Skeggs (1988, 1991, 1997) and Bates and Riseborough (1993) examined the way in which students' experiences in FE served to reproduce class-based orientations towards waged labour. This work examined the way in which educational processes contributed to the formation of learners' dispositions, serving to locate individuals in particular class and occupational positions, albeit recognizing that these were mediated by race and gender. The work of Bates (1991) and Skeggs (1988, 1997) on domestic apprenticeships of young women on caring courses emphasized the gendered processes involved in the reproduction of class relations (and see Colley, 2006; Preston, 2003). To reiterate, it is important to recognize that the formation of class relations is necessarily gendered and raced. Skeggs (1997) for example has written about the formation of a caring self that coincides with the formation of a particular kind of white working-class femininity that serves to reproduce class and gendered relations.

Lived experience

In this section the lived experience of 16–19-year-olds within the sector will be addressed. It is important to distinguish the experiences of this group from that of older students who are also differentiated in a number of important ways. Access students have historically experienced their encounter with further education as an epiphany – a real transformation of their identities and of their understanding of the wider social formation. Edwards' (1993) work stands as an example of this. It is however necessary to recognize the continuities between the strategies used by older students to survive and engage with the sector and those present within the school system (see for example Avis, 1996c, 1997).

Whilst recognizing the differentiations found amongst 16–19-year-olds in further education, a consistent feature of the research has been that such learners find further education offers a more adult context in which to learn and study. They often claim that they are treated in a more adult manner and that this is one of the features of the sector they value (see Ainley and Bailey, 1997; Attwood *et al.*, 2003, 2004; Avis, 1991b; Bates, 1991; Bathmaker, 2001; Ecclestone, 2002). Despite changes that have put in place enhanced systems of accountability and have sought to attach greater responsibility to teachers for student progression, in Ainley and Bailey's (1997) study students still considered themselves to be responsible for success or failure. Bathmaker (2001) found similar patterns in her study of GNVQ foundation students. In addition she discussed an 'unwritten alliance' between staff and students whereby staff would offer additional help and support to students who appeared willing and were prepared to make an effort (and see Avis *et al.*, 2002). There is a resonance here with Brown's (1987) 'ordinary kids' who were prepared to buy into the teaching exchange, to do enough provided this offered a route to respectable working-class jobs.

Somewhat paradoxically, where students encountered teaching relations that reminded them of school resistance to infantalization sometimes emerged (Avis, 1984; Bathmaker and Avis, forthcoming; Stafford, 1991). Young people carry into college a range of orientations that influences the way in which they approach their studies. Some years ago Lesley Haddon (1983) drew attention to the social uses students made of college as a locale to meet friends and extend their social lives. Such orientations are unchanged and remain in place (and see Avis, 1991b).

For those students following vocational pathways the adult feel of further education is deepened through their engagement in practical activities as well as their involvement with the real world of work (Avis, 1984; Bates, 1991; Skeggs, 1991). Such engagements conspire with the ongoing formation of subjective dispositions towards waged labour that are not only linked to class but also to race, sexuality and the continuous formation of masculinity and femininity (Avis, 1984; Bates, 1991; Haywood and Mac An Ghaill, 1997; Mac An Ghaill, 1999; Skeggs, 1991, 1997). Mac An Ghaill has, for example, discussed the articulation of sexuality amongst trainees following a modern apprenticeship and the manner in which this feeds into identity as well as in particular the construction of work-based identities. Similarly Bates (1991) and Skeggs (1991, 1997) in studies of youth training schemes and caring courses located within further education explored the responses of young women to caring. They examined the way in which these constructed a domestic apprenticeship in which the formation of sexuality and femininity played an important role. It is important to recognize that these processes are not straight-forward and that learner agency was expressed in a number of ways. For example, sexuality (as in the case of Mac An Ghaill and Skeggs' students) would be marshalled to either resist or accommodate, or even create diversions that constituted course survival strategies. In addition for many students following vocational pathways the most valued aspects of their college experience were those oriented towards vocational practice. In many cases where work placements were provided these offered students a sense of worth and a real engagement with the world of adult labour. Such engagements served to validate practical over mental labour. Skeggs (1997), for example, discussed the manner in which her students inverted the validation of mental and manual labour so as to place greater value on the latter. Whilst current conditions may cloud these relations, linking them to forms of technicism, these patterns nevertheless remain in place. The mental–manual divide as in previous and current configurations serves an important role in the formation of class differentiation.

Learners have followed a variety of trajectories and adopted numerous orientations to post-compulsory education. Some have adopted a critical stance and politicized orientation towards the curriculum that served to debunk the claimed objectivity of knowledge (Avis, 1991b; Bloomer, 1997; Hollands, 1990). However, such politicized orientations seem to be relatively rare and to have become increasingly so in recent years. Ecclestone (2002) in her study of GNVQ students suggests that her learners tended to distance themselves from critical practices, viewing these as irrelevant and over-academicized knowledge, preferring instead to focus on practical aspects. She argued that it was unreasonable to expect learners to adopt the sorts of autonomy which underpinned radical practice and that rather they should be seen as passing through varying types of autonomy which could lead to more radical forms. Changes in participation rates and an increasingly performative attitude towards education, allied to a difficult youth labour market, encourage both instrumentalism and a technicization of learning. This is in part reflected in the emphasis placed upon individualization, the personalization of learning and an outcome-oriented prescriptive curriculum (Ecclestone, 2002).

From reproduction to learning cultures

Work that adopted a reproductive stance has been criticized for its failure to engage seriously with the processes and practices of learning. In much of this work an orientation towards educational practice often appears as an afterthought and is far less developed than the analysis of reproduction or indeed resistance. Paul Willis's (1977) work provides an example, but his recent work (2004) has attempted to address practice more seriously. Other writers such as Apple and Giroux have consistently attempted to draw together radical, if not neo-marxist analysis, with the development of critical educational practices within school (Beane and Apple, 1999; Giroux, 1992). Despite this work, in the closing years of the twentieth century class and structural analyses of education became increasingly marginalized (see Dolby and Dimitriadis, 2004 for discussion). This is partly a result of changes in the socio-economic context as well as claims that social relations have become far more fluid and therefore structural analyses have lost something of their heuristic value. The marginalization of class is also a consequence of changes in the way in which writers have sought to examine educational processes so as to acknowledge complexity and specificity at an institutional as well as individual level. The strength of past theories of social reproduction was that these firmly located education within capitalist relations, the formation of labour power and social structure. These insights are under-played in recent analyses that have taken a culturalist direction as well as those that sideline class analysis, castigating these former theories for their determinism and failure to recognize agency – whether it be that of teachers or indeed learners.

Gewirtz and Cribb (2003) argue that after the 1970s and 1980s the sociology of education shifted away from grand theorizing characteristic of reproduction theories as well as from the centrality placed on class, leading towards:

> more complex, differentiated and context-sensitive forms of theorising. These more differentiated approaches have sought to describe and explain local difference and complexity. In particular, in rejecting the universalism and determinism characteristic of the earlier theories the newer approaches have sought to unpack the ways in which processes of social reproduction work differently at different times and in different social locations for different constitu-encies. (p. 244)

Gewirtz and Cribb suggest these moves have arisen as a consequence of three developments: disputes within the sociology of
education, socio-economic changes and, third, the rise of post-
structuralism (2003, p. 245). The latter, through the challenge it
posed to grand theorizing and reproduction theory, encouraged
the development of analyses that moved away from those
based 'upon *episteme* (analytical, scientific knowledge)' to those
'based upon *phronesis* (practical judgement or wisdom)' (2003,
p. 247; and see Gewirtz, 2004). The current interest in learning
cultures reflects this move. There is an attempt to take account
of the complexity of educational relations, to recognize learner
agency as well as to seriously engage with educational practice
in progressive ways.

Much current work claims to be rooted within a Bourdieuian
analysis that emphasizes young people's orientation to
knowledge and learning cultures. These contrast with accounts
that rest comfortably with reproduction theory and were
discussed earlier. In the recent work of Hodkinson, Bloomer,
Ball *et al.*, we are provided with far more nuanced accounts
of learners' experiences (Ball *et al.*, 2000; Bloomer, 1997;
Bloomer and Hodkinson, 1999; Hodkinson, Sparkes, and
Hodkinson, 1996). These authors are at pains to acknowledge
the structural basis of class inequality that impacts upon and
is reconstituted within education, albeit mediated through the
structures of race and gender. These structural processes seem
to 'recede into the background' whilst those that relate to
individualization are brought to the foreground.

> The culture and ideology of individualism interpenetrates, feeds
> and is fed by – social changes which encourage greater reflexivity
> and individualization. Thus, here we want to signal the way in
> which the political and economic culture of neo-liberalism, of the
> market, with its stress on individualism, connects with 'individuali-
> zation' changes in social identity and social attachments. Working
> together, the ideology of economic individualism and individu-
> alization as a reflexive project of identity formation, mute and
> obscure the continuing class-based nature of structural inequalities.
> 'Class differences and family connections are not really annulled ...
> they recede into the background relative to the newly emerging

"center" of the biographical life plan'. (Beck 1992, p. 131) (Ball *et al.* 2000, p. 3)

Paradoxically, there is a link between the bracketing of structural issues and the theoretical and methodological basis of the above work, in as much as it is located within a social, economic and cultural context thought to have undergone qualitative changes over the last 20 or 30 years (Gleeson and Keep, 2004). Beck is drawn on approvingly, as is the work of Castells and Giddens in making sense of the new social and economic conditions. Much of this current work examines young people's orientations to further education, having an ethnographic focus. It draws upon case study analysis, seeking to develop an account that addresses the narrative production of individual identity, albeit set within a cultural and structural location (see, Bloomer, 1997; Bloomer and Hodkinson, 1999; (JVET), 2003; Lawy, 2003, 2004).

This type of analysis rests with a particular understanding of the social formation, one located within conditions of reflexive modernity, which carries with it the growth of individualization. The self is seen as a reflexive project – we construct narratives of our self-identity that place us in particular social relations (Giddens, 1991). Ball *et al.* echo notions of reflexive modernity that see identity as not only a social production but also as part of a reflexive project. The idea of 'choice biographies' is drawn upon:

In our view, learning is about social biographies and identities rather than human capital. It is about self-realisation rather than futurity. It is about meaning and difference, about struggle, disappointment and imagination. It is located in social participation as well as in the heads of individuals (2000, pp. 9–10)

Although Ball *et al.* recognize the importance of class difference, and by default reproductive or formative processes that (re)constitute inequality, they stress that learners negotiate lifestyle choices from amongst a diversity of options:

Again the abstract 'individualisations' of Beck and Giddens are confronted by the practicalities of family and custom, and the

fixities of labour market structures and the demand for qualifications. However, in the same way the continuing importance
of class differences have to be set against and take into account
the agency and activism of the young people portrayed here. (2000,
p. 40)

Ball *et al.* refer approvingly to Hodkinson's work in their
consideration of young people's orientation to education, citing
pragmatic rationality and allied notions of career (Hodkinson *et
al.*, 1996; and see Bloomer, 1997, 2001). The case study orientation of Ball *et al.*, whilst echoing Bloomer and Hodkinson,
places a greater emphasis upon class processes, a theme
running throughout Ball's work (2003, 2004). In Bloomer
and Hodkinson's (2001) analyses the focus is upon individual
learners. When class is addressed, it is as if they seek to trace
back from the outcomes of educative and social processes to an
analysis of class dispositions and the impact of various forms of
capital. This can be seen in one of their case studies and their
discussion of respondents (Tamsin and Daniel), whose current
position is used to enable a discussion of cultural capital and
its movement over time (Bloomer and Hodkinson, 2001). An
alternative way of exploring this data would be to view these
young people not only as classed but as actively (re)producing
class throughout their educative and social experiences.

Despite their apparent radicalism the early analyses of
Bloomer and Hodkinson were rooted within symbolic interactionism from where notions of career were drawn (Bloomer,
1997; Hodkinson *et al.*, 1996). This is reflected in the idea that
learning should be thought of as a process of becoming as
well as of transformation (Bloomer, 1997, 2001; Bloomer and
Hodkinson, 2001; Hodkinson and Bloomer, 2000). Bloomer
and Hodkinson, describing their notion of learning culture and
transformation, write:

Learning careers constitute both continuity and change, although
the balance between them may differ markedly from case to case,
from time to time and from situation to situation. For this reason we
have adopted the term transformation, to describe the development
of learning careers, although transformations ... are often neither

sudden nor dramatic, and may take many forms. They are not prede-
termined, although they are orientated by the habitus and the former
life. (2001, p. 132)

Symbolic interactionist understandings of 'becoming' imply
a transformation of the way we think of ourselves, our
relationship to knowledge and to the social formation. A
view of transformation rooted in symbolic interactionism is
qualitatively different from that present within, for example,
Marxism. Hodkinson, Bloomer, James and others have taken
these concepts, developing their analyses further in an examination of learning and teaching cultures in further education
(Bloomer, 2000; James and Bloomer, 2001; JVET, 2004).
Whilst this work is grounded in and has an affinity with understandings of the socio-economic context that draws upon Beck
and Gidden's work on reflexive modernity and the risk society,
they all draw heavily upon Bourdieuian theorizations.
   Bloomer writes:

Transformations in learning careers are complex and cannot be
properly represented by crude causal models, whether sociological
or psychological ... I have argued that, for the complexities of these
processes to be made apparent, the *situatedness* of knowledge and
learning, the position of the learner, the relationality of learning and
identity must be fully recognised. (2002, p. 443)

Such ideas are reflected in the theoretical discussions of James,
Diment, Hodkinson and Colley in the *Transforming Learning
Cultures in Further Education Project* (see Colley *et al.*, 2003;
Hodkinson and James, 2003; James, 2002; James and Diment,
2003). This work predicated upon cultural understandings of
learning draws from three theoretical resources to justify its
approach. First, an interdisciplinary argument suggests disciplinary approaches are often reductive as they can close down
analysis and become unduly restrictive.

We can choose to put learning as a set of practices to be understood,
explained or transformed, at the centre of our work. Whereas,
someone operating from more of a disciplinary position might begin

with established classificatory practices – perhaps seeing a learning situation as symptomatic of particular cognitive styles, information processing or policy implementation. (James and Diment, 2003, p. 408)

Interdisciplinarity uncovers the complexity of educational and social relations that bear upon learning cultures. This position sits closely with their second theoretical resource, Bourdieu's theory of practice (James, 2002). They draw upon a range of conceptual tools from Bourdieu, amongst which are habitus and field.

[Habitus] 'names the characteristic dispositions of the social subject. It is indicated in the bearing of the body and in deeply ingrained habits of behaviour, feeling, thought' (Lovell, 2000, p. 27). Habitus engages with the field, which is conceptualised as 'a structured system of social relations, at micro and macro level, rather like a field of forces in which positions are defined ... in relation to each other' (James and Bloomer 2001, p. 5). It is the dialectical nature of the relationship between habitus and field that helps the researcher to avoid constructing 'reified "types" or "categories"'. (James and Bloomer 2001, p. 5) (quoted in James and Diment, 2003, p. 409)

Bourdieuian tools provide an important conceptual resource in attempting to grasp the complexity of social, economic and educational relations. They refuse a simple duality between agency and structure and offer a way to develop nuanced and complex accounts of learning cultures. Pivotally, they encourage reflexivity and an orientation to learning that places it in a broader context than is usual, facilitating analyses that understand learning and teaching primarily as 'social and cultural rather than as individual or technical activities' (Colley et al., 2003, p. 472). This rests with the third resource underpinning the work of these authors, Lave and Wenger's (1991) notion of situated learning and its participatory nature. This offers a social theory of learning, understood not in terms of the acquisition of knowledge but rather as a process of social participation – a process of becoming through which learners dialectically construct identity. James and Diment comment on Lave and Wenger's understanding of transformation:

> The work of Lave and Wenger and collaborators is helpful on a number of fronts, including the powerful idea that transformation is cultural – that it is both a personal and a situational or structural process. (2003, p. 411)

This third theoretical resource and the Bourdieuian conceptualizations refer back to interdisciplinarity, as well as to the roots of Bloomer and Hodkinson's work within symbolic interactionism. To reiterate, within symbolic interactionism notions of identity are intimately tied to educational processes, with pedagogic experiences offering transformative possibilities. However, these derive from individual experiences, albeit socially and culturally located within educational processes that themselves are involved in a kind of 'transcendental violence' that leads the learner to modify who and what they are (Biesta, 2004).

Reflections

Given the undoubted strengths of the preceding arguments, why is it that I feel uneasy about these analyses? After all the authors are at pains to produce a fully social and relational account of learning and teaching cultures. Perhaps I am guilty of the substantialist thinking that Hodkinson and James castigate.

> Bourdieu contrasts *relational* with *substantialist* thinking: the latter treats the preferences and activities of individuals or groups as if they indicate an essence, whilst the former sees them as instances of the intersection of relationships and positions in social space. (Hodkinson and James, 2003, p. 394)

There are a number of tensions that need to be explored. There is an affinity between the ideational context reflected in current social theory and the socio-economic environment within which the above is located. Paradoxically, the very complexity of the analysis pushes it towards individualization in two senses. First, towards a model rooted within the contemporary social theories of Beck, Giddens and Castell, who explore the loss of collectivity and the way in which class and inequality is clouded by individualization. This loss of collectivity derives from the current socio-economic context. Savage (2003) in his review of Ball (2003) offers a slightly different position on these issues, arguing that class has not so much become occluded, but that middle-class notions of individualism have become hegemonic. The middle class has become the 'universal-particular class'. That is to say Beckian notions of individualization become articulated to the bourgeois possessive individual with structural relations of power and inequality becoming obscured. Such an analysis draws attention to questions of power and ideology and the manner in which our understanding of the social formation impacts upon analysis (see, Reay, 2003). Within some of the *Transforming Learning Cultures* (*TLC*) work class, ethnicity and gender are used ritualistically. The citation of the trilogy is used to mark an awareness of structural relations. But paradoxically, such relations become less visible, and as far as class is concerned there is not a strong sense of the way in which 'class gets done'.

> [Class] is an identity based upon modes of being and becoming and forms of distinction that are realised and reproduced in specific social locations. We 'think' and are 'thought by' class. It is about being something and not being something else. It is relational. Class is also a trajectory, a path through space and time, a 'history of transactions'. We are not always the same or always able to be the same, as the world around us changes. 'Real world classes are constantly being constructed around us, people are constantly doing class'. (Connell cited in Ball, 2004, p. 7)

Perhaps we should think about educational processes more directly in terms of the formation and reproduction of class differences as well as inequality.

A second tension surrounds a notion of individualization

tied to identity, which veers towards seeing the individual as the basis for the development of identity. What is understated is an understanding of the way labour power is being formed, as well as the mode in which capitalist relations are being secured (but see Gleeson and Keep, 2004; Gleeson *et al.*, 2005). Lauder and Brown (2003) draw attention to the manner in which the neo-liberal state attempts to reconfigure and re-form class relations, providing a contextualization for processes of individualization. Individual action planning, the personalization and allied commodification of the curriculum, all of which is a feature of the learning and skills sector, sits comfortably with these processes. This type of examination calls for a political analysis of educative processes with the formation of identity being but one strand. Although current work within the *TLC project* places identity formation within its social and cultural context, a politicized analysis could be pushed much further. Such an analysis is partly compromised by the very basis of the project and its concern to intervene within the sector to transform learning and teaching cultures. There is a significant tension within this work that seeks to intervene to improve practice and involve users, arising from a state-driven imperative to conjure solutions to the day-to-day problems of practitioners (but see Hodkinson, 2005). This is reflected in the tension between theorized understandings and suggestions for the improvement of practice. There is an attempt to broaden the understanding of teaching and learning to acknowledge its location within social and cultural processes (see Hodkinson and James, 2003; James, 2004). Whilst the project's theoretical framework adopts a sophisticated understanding of further education, it is nevertheless constrained by the previous concerns. This is reflected in tensions surrounding the notion of habitus.

Earlier I noted James and Diment's distinction between habitus and field; to reiterate:

> [Habitus] 'names the characteristic dispositions of the social subject. It is indicated in the bearing of the body and in deeply ingrained habits of behaviour, feeling, thought' (Lovell, 2000, p. 27). Habitus

engages with the field, which is conceptualised as 'a structured system of social relations, at micro and macro level, rather like a field of forces in which positions are defined ... in relation to each other'. (James and Bloomer 2001, p. 5) (quoted in James and Diment, 2003, p. 409)

It is at the level of field that structure enters into a dialectical relationship with habitus. Habitus in the form of cultural dispositions impacts on the way in which learners make sense of educational relations and is allied to college culture through the idea of institutional habitus (see Hodkinson and Bloomer, 2000). These forms of habitus may align or be in contradiction with one or other gaining ascendancy. Habitus emphasizes the cultural and dispositional, and can lead to marginalization of the structural, in as much as this is reflected within the field, which is seen to be socially and culturally constituted. There is a tendency to downplay material relations. Perhaps the dialectic should start with the field of power and then examine habitus for the way in which 'class gets done', is worked on and reconstituted. As with contemporary theorizing, which stresses complexity and indeterminacy, structural and material relations can come to be seen as the backdrop to education.

An emphasis upon learning and improvement can easily veer towards a cultural analysis that avoids significant social, economic and political questions. How do we challenge and interrupt the pervasiveness of capitalist education? Will trans-formations of learning and teaching cultures generate the forms of civic engagement that Gleeson calls for (Gleeson and Keep, 2004; Gleeson *et al.*, 2005)? Gleeson *et al.* writing on the 'restorying' of professionalism note:

It is also contingent on the restoration of wider forms of democratic governance and accountability which grow out of cultural capital and citizenship, which transcend market narratives and consumerist concerns (Bourdieu and Wacquant, 1992). If part of this process involves democratic governance it is also dependent on more trans-parent forms of plurality, contestation and accountability at the centre of the public sphere ... Central to this process is a balancing of 'agreement making' (Nixon and Ranson, 1997) between government, professional and local communities concerning the objectives, strategies and forms of accountability that form part of a wider democratic conversation. (2005, p. 456)

It is important to recognize, as do Hodkinson and James (2003, p. 398), that *TLC* is an interdisciplinary project, with various writers stressing and developing slightly different analyses. Thus, for example, the work of Colley *et al.* (2003), Wahlberg and Gleeson (2003) place a greater emphasis on structural relations (and see Colley and Hodkinson, 2001).

It is important to consider the way in which the structural is conceived. For Bourdieu, structural relations derive from unequal positions and are reproduced through enacted and embodied practices. There is a dialectical relation between agency and structure with any clear-cut simplistic demarcations being inappropriate. However, behind constructions of the social structure lie the interests of particular social groups. Savage's analysis points towards the hegemony of middle-class interests in the construction of individualization.

An awareness of social structure as well as the patterning of social inequality, not only along the lines of class but also gender and race, needs to be placed in the foreground. There are a number of ways this could be done. Ball *et al.* (2000) adopted a Weberian approach that recognizes the differential interests of various groups. Such an analysis opens up questions of power, politics and interest but could easily be appropriated by reformist politics. For example, New Labour's reforms aim to create a just society by challenging unfairness and elitism, without challenging capitalist relations (Brown, 2000). Without such a challenge these analyses are rendered complicit with existing social and economic relations and adopt a reformist hue. To overcome this we need analyses that recognize the manner in which social antagonisms are embedded in social and educational relations and that fundamentally different and conflictual interests exist. What would an analysis of further education that sought to incorporate social antagonism look like? Such an analysis could be viewed as essentialist and one that misses the complexity of social relations. The problem with an analysis that emphasizes social antagonism is that it creates difficulties for college-based interventions. Gleeson *et al.*'s concern with the restoration of the civic sphere and 'agreement making' goes some way to address these anxieties. However, this type of analysis can veer towards a Weberian pluralism as well as incorporating the difficulties of a Habermasian approach. Rikowski's (1999) notion of 'human made capital' is valuable; it alerts us to the need to interrogate practices for their contradictions and underlying interests. It also points towards a notion of struggle, not only external but within ourselves. There is also the question of the way in which social antagonism is played out in classroom relations. Questions here focus on the manner in which class relations, mediated by gender and ethnicity, articulate to the reproduction of labour power and inequality. This points towards an analysis rooted in a political economy of educational relations working with a different notion of transformation, anticipated earlier but that extends from a transformation of learner and teacher identity through to social and political relations. It opens up a politicized analysis that challenges the hegemony of capitalist interests and interrogates class-based practices. This potentiality is present within the *TLC* project but its development calls for a move into a broader political terrain that challenges the modernizing project of New Labour.

Work that explores young people's educative experiences needs to place learning cultures within a wider context that can address not only the manner in which class identities are formed, reproduced, and interrupted within further education but also to seriously examine the relationship of this with the formation of particular types of masculinity, femininity and sexuality. It is here that the work of Bates, Skeggs and Mac An Ghaill are important, as well as Colley's (2006) more recent work. In a similar manner Gillborn (2005, 2006), Youdell (2003) and Preston (2003) remind us of related processes that articulate with the construction of whiteness, the othering of black youth as well as the formation of an educational system predicated in Gillborn's words on 'white supremacy'. A supremacy that is marked by the patterning of educational outcomes – we might also add that this supremacy also reflects class processes.

Conclusion

Whilst analyses of reflexive modernity capture the ongoing transformation and complexity of social and economic relations, they tend to move towards a model of individualization that is politically disabling. Social and economic transformation forms the backdrop to studies of further education, with earlier work emphasizing the relationship between pedagogic experience and reproduction of labour and capitalist relations. More recent work reflects the complexity of educational relations found within theories of reflexive modernization. The danger is that this work bears an ambivalent relation to individualization and through its desire to refuse determinist and essentialist accounts fails to develop a sufficiently politicized analysis. Such an analysis would retain the complexity of educational and social relations but would relate these to 'capitalist education'. Processes of individualization are deeply ideological; whilst having the appearance of autonomy they are nevertheless deeply embedded within capitalist relations and the ongoing formation/reproduction of labour power. A fully politicized account of further education necessitates a recognition of the antagonistic relations present within education and the social formation, Rikowski's (1999) work points towards the way these are internalized. The radicalism of the *TLC* project is understated by its analysis of the relationship between education and capital and its failure to stress the dispositional basis of the ongoing production of labour power. Class-based struggles and differential interests criss-cross education and need to be placed in the foreground, otherwise New Labour's understanding of elitism and inequality will occupy this space and support a modernized capitalist education. The alternative is the restoration of a radical educational politics that extends and embraces social relations outside education and which places in a central position social antagonism and the struggle for social justice.

Notes

1 A four-year ESRC study, part of the *Teaching and Learning Research programme*. It 'takes a cultural approach to learning. Its core aims are to:
   - deepen understanding of the complexities of learning;
   - identify, implement and evaluate strategies for the improvement of learning opportunities;
   - set in place an enhanced and lasting capacity among practitioners for enquiry into FE practice.' (Hodkinson and James, 2003, pp. 389–90)
2 See Chapter 3 Note 2 for level descriptors.

5

Teachers and the transformation of practice

It is now commonplace to bemoan the conditions faced by those working in education. The success of the new right in the 1970s and 1980s in transforming educational relations has carried in its wake new patterns of accountability, the commodification of education and the intensification of waged labour, marked by the rush towards performance indicators and efficiency gains (Avis *et al.*, 1996; Education Group II, 1991). All of these have been taken up enthusiastically and extended by New Labour in recent years. Accounts of these conditions abound and have been linked with changes in the nature of teacher professionalism (see for example Menter *et al.*, 1997). Much of the English research has illustrated the anti-educational consequences of the Thatcherite years and, latterly, has challenged those aspects of New Labour policy that are in continuity with it (Avis, 1998; Hatcher, 1997). Resting alongside these accounts lie studies commissioned by teacher unions to examine workloads and stress levels (see for example Batten and Skinner, 1997; Earley, 1994; Kinman, 1996). These studies have brought to light the anti-educational consequences of an overstressed and overworked profession.

This chapter examines a number of issues concerning the nature of teaching and learning in the English post-compulsory sector and reflects changes found throughout the system from school to higher education. These changes are not exclusive to England, being reflected in societies that have experienced educational polices shaped by the new right in conjunction with modernizing tendencies which carry in their wake moves towards managerialism. These changes are set in a context of fiscal rectitude as well as the rewriting of what it is to be a state professional (see for example Apple, 1996). This chapter considers the lived experience of teachers and sets this against the educational discourse that informs change. This has become particularly important in the context of New Labour. With Thatcherism it was relatively easy to criticize the banalities and distortions embedded in market-based educational policies (Avis *et al.*, 1996; Ball, 1993; Education Group II, 1991). It was clear that recourse to the market hid significant class-based processes that secured the interests of middle-class constituencies and served to deepen educational as well as social inequalities (Fabian Commission, 2006; Joseph Rowntree Foundation, 1995). With New Labour there is a shift from the 'politics' of conflict towards a serious attempt to secure a new educational and social settlement, one that uses as its leitmotiv empowerment, social cohesion and inclusion as well as individual responsibility (see Rustin, 1997). Whilst the Conservatives favoured institutional competition, under New Labour there is a stated aspiration to move towards partnership. In the government's response to the Kennedy Report (1997) it states:

> The government believes that the excessive emphasis in the past on market competition has inhibited collaboration; and that strong partnerships are now needed to develop efficient local strategies for learning. (DfEE, 1998c, p. 9) [and see THES, 1998, p. 10]

Although such an aspiration remains in place and is used rhetorically, institutional competition continues to be a significant feature of education (DfES, 2006). The Foster Review, which examined the current state of further education, commenting on the problem of post-incorporation stated:

> [Isolating] individual teaching institutions from each other in a potentially counter-productive competitive environment, reducing the opportunities for collaborative cost sharing, trans-provider learning

pathways and the provision of learner centred advice and guidance. (Foster, 2005, p. 11)

And argued that:

These consequences can be mitigated without losing the benefits of incorporation. (Foster, 2005, p. 11)

Such moves take place under the surveillance of the contracting state through systems of accountability allied to performance management that set the terrain on which institutions operate, with power resting securely with the state (Ainley and Bailey, 1997). The appropriateness of notions of partnership is a moot point, organizations such as the LSC are placed in a junior and subordinate position, as are the colleges whose provision the LSC funds (Jones, 2004). Resting alongside New Labour's notions of partnership remains an unquestioned acceptance of market and capitalist relations, which are taken as axiomatic.

Chantall Mouffe writing in *New Times* worries about the loss of politics that flows from New Labour's consensual strategy:

A wide consensus seems to have been established about the irrelevancies of the categories, 'left' and 'right', and the dinosaurs who still use them, who do not understand the consequences of globalisation in the world today. The notion of a 'radical centre' is the trademark of new Labour.

I worry about the consequences of this. Firstly, new Labour are not attempting anything radical, having seemingly adopted wholesale a 'triangulation strategy' originally designed for Clinton's America: that is taking up the goals and slogans of both left and right in order to create a centre comprising the demands of both. (1998, p. 6)

The construction of a consensual politics built around the apparent collapse of the distinction between left and right is pivotal to an understanding of the changes impacting upon post-compulsory education that seek to redefine patterns of teaching and learning. The work emanating from social theorists such as Giddens as well as left of centre think tanks such as the Institute of Public Policy Research (IPPR) and Demos accept the collapse of this distinction. Giddens writes:

> Many conservatives are now active radicals in respect of that very phenomenon which previously they held most dear – tradition. 'Away with the fossils we have inherited from the past': where is such a sentiment most commonly to be heard? Not on the left, but on the right.
>
> Conservatism become radical here confronts socialism become conservative ... socialists have mostly been thrown back on the defensive, their position in the 'vanguard of history' reduced to the more modest task of protecting welfare institutions. (1994, p. 2)

In Demos we encounter a similar thrust. Chris Ham writing about the health service:

> As the regulator, government will need to ensure that a proper balance is struck between planning and competition ... The middle way between planning and competition is called contestability.
>
> The challenge is to move beyond traditional dichotomies of public versus private, collective versus individual responsibility, planning versus markets, and centralisation versus decentralisation. A new synthesis is needed in which government does better by doing less. (1996, p. 10)

There is here a continuity with an older social democratic politics, in part reflected in notions of social inclusion which have a resonance with older ideas of equal opportunity and meritocracy. But what is new in the current conjuncture is the way in which such arguments have become oriented to an understanding of economic and social change and the needs that flow from these that seek to reorganize professional identity and to destabilize opposition to policy.

Trust

Chapter 2 discussed the competitiveness settlement that incorporates a specific understanding of work relations and the economy. A number of associations are developed within this argument. A high skills economy is inextricably tied to high wages and high-trust work relations. It is through the exercise of skills and knowledge that workers create value-added 'products'. Knowledge and its manipulation becomes pivotal to attaining competitive advantage. It is within this context and through the continuous exercise of a range of transferable and intellective skills that the worker will be enabled to keep pace with the rapidity of social and economic change. Michael Young suggests:

> The demands of work will therefore be increasingly opaque to direct experience and more and more dependent *on those involved developing new concepts, skills and knowledge*. These combinations of skill and knowledge are referred to by a variety of terms such as 'connective', 'conceptual' or 'intellective'. [My emphasis] (1998b, p. 199)

It is at this juncture that those skills associated with the symbolic analyst come into play and where creativity is to emerge (Reich, 1991). However, working conditions marked by hierarchical and segmented relations will fail to generate work-based cultures that lend themselves to creative endeavour. Whereas work based on teamwork, collective problem solving and non-hierarchical relations will be able to utilize the intellective skills of the worker. In order to facilitate such a process relationships that are based on trust and enable risk taking need to be established. It is through such a process that the worker is 'freed' to express creativity and contribute towards collective problem solving. Trust becomes a prerequisite for the knowledge worker, for without it risks will not be taken and new ideas remain unexpressed, hindering the development of competitiveness and continuous improvement. These ideas are not attached to any particular part of the economy but can be generalized throughout as well as across the public/private divide.

In education such an analysis would suggest that high-skill, high-trust relations could set the context in which innovatory practices develop. The education system is after all charged with developing the knowledge workers of the future who will be labouring, it is asserted, in high-trust, high-waged employment. This argument would suggest the need to develop a re-formed teacher professionalism, one that accords with the new conditions of risk and uncertainty within which the economy and education is set.

These arguments, when accented towards educational practice both open up and close off particular forms of professional identity; the traditional professional who has invested in an identity as a subject specialist being set against the pedagogue who facilitates learning. If, in the past, the subject specialist was dominant the weighting of the terms have now been reversed – facilitating learning becomes pivotal with subject specialism becoming secondary. Such moves carry with them a shift in the identities available to teachers. Wahlberg and Gleeson, in a recent study, discuss the ambiguity surrounding business studies tutors' status and relationship to their originating disciplines:

> Discussion among tutors about 'earlier times', when 'professional' staff came in to teach on business courses is revealing. Reference is made to the accountants' still being 'like that' ... they are seen as and will always remain 'accountants'. Harry ... by contrast feels that he used to be 'an economist', then a lecturer, but that one of the changes that has occurred recently is that he has become 'a teacher'.
>
> ... [George] points out that 'with the younger kids' he is now hardly a teacher, and feels more like a welfare officer or social worker. (Walhberg and Gleeson, 2003, p. 437)

In part such identity shifts are based on a recognition of the changing constituencies that FE addresses, or at least an interpretation of the complexity of social and economic processes that bear upon the sector, which attempt to re-form social relations. In such a milieu pedagogic skills have been rearticulated in a manner that accents the enabling of learning over specific disciplinary skills. The rapidity of technological change places a premium upon the development of mode 2 knowledge, one that is situational and tied to particular contexts. Whilst at the time of writing there is a concern with subject specialist pedagogy this is nevertheless set within the former discourse that prioritizes the facilitation of learning. The Lifelong Learning UK (LLUK) standards state in relation to Domain B – specialist area and its pedagogy:

> **Teachers with QTLS value:**
> Maintenance of secure and current knowledge and understanding of own specialist area.
> The enthusing and motivating of learners in own specialist area.
> Own role and responsibilities as a specialist teacher.
> Development of good practice in own specialist area.
> (LLUK, 2006, BS 1, BS 2, BS 3, BS 4)

There is another paradox, the concern with trust and creativity and the encouragement of apparently progressive models of educational practice rest uneasily with the conditions within which teachers labour as well as the pedagogic context in which they work.

Lived experience

> 'We want to give our students something extraordinary in their lives,' says Tony Henry. This apparent largesse is despite – or perhaps because of East Birmingham college having one of the lowest unit costs in the sector. 'We can fund it because of the cost efficiency of the "Charles Handy model" we are pursuing in our staffing – one-third permanent staff, one-third agency staff and one-third portfolio workers. (*FE Now!* 1997, p. 9)

The above is drawn from a page advertisement sponsored by Education Lecturing Services (ELS), an employment agency. In it a college principle is describing the efficiencies that might enable the travel costs of students on work experience in the US to be met. The passage is significant in that it epitomizes a number of elements that have refigured teaching and learning within further education. It refers to the work of management guru Charles Handy, celebrates new work relations that create a leaner, fitter organization, and most importantly attempts to set this within a learner-centred framework. There is a direct continuity with Blairism that similarly celebrates the work of Handy and other management gurus (Beckett, 2005). In another publication Henry cites approvingly a statement from a chief executive of a computer company, which also resonates with Blairism:

> Students are the most important visitors on our premises. They are not dependent on us, we are dependent on them. They are not interruptions of our work, they are the purpose of it. They are not outsiders of our business, they are part of it. We are not doing them a service by serving them, they are doing us a favour by giving us an opportunity to do so. (Henry, 1994, p. 213)

In the same article in a parody of Althusser (1972, p. 261) Henry describes teaching as a heroic activity:

> The new heroines and heroes of the organisation are the tutors. They are the ones who will be able to deliver the information demanded by the recurrent funding methodology and the student-tracking demanded by the funding council. They will be involved in intensive training and will be rewarded for the arduous task that they will have in the new structure. How will all this be paid for? By the redistribution of resources from middle and senior management. (Henry, 1994, p. 216)

Interestingly enough our heroic figures will be distracted from pedagogic concerns and become embroiled in administration. Ainley and Bailey's study confirmed the long-standing finding that main grade lecturers resented the growth of their administrative workload:

> ... at least at the time we interviewed members of the colleges' staff, there were unanimous complaints from the main-grade teachers that the administrative load was overwhelming and they were drowning under paperwork. (1997, p. 62)

And later they commented:

The increased work load was not resented for itself but because it detracted from what interviewees saw as the essential public service that the college was supposed to provide. (1997, p. 67)

In many respects the findings in this study echo those of much of the current and earlier work on further education (Venables, 1967). Elliott writes:

The speed and scope of change is unprecedented. Lecturers have experienced acute loss of control of their work situation ... There is a real tension in colleges between the management-imposed imperatives of satisfying quantitative performance indicators, and lecturers' conceptions and priorities based upon their value judgements. (1996a, p. 60)

For many teachers these new conditions are less than healthy. The Natfhe research on stress is indicative of these tendencies (Batten and Skinner, 1997; Earley, 1994; Kinman, 1996). Ainley and Bailey found those new to teaching in FE were more ready to accommodate to the condition in which they found themselves (and see Avis, Bathmaker and Parsons, 2002; Wahlberg and Gleeson, 2003). In a process akin to that discussed by Gouldner (1968), changes in the management regime were more readily accommodated by new staff than those from an earlier time. Amongst the latter group a number would seek to change their job or take early retirement (see Gleeson, 2001). Within FE, those lecturers committed to teaching and who attempt to manage the increased administrative workload may find themselves exhausted. James and Diment's (2003) notion of underground learning illustrates this. Using an example from their research, they illustrate the way in which a particular task can be understood differently by those involved. For management a particular lecturer's (Gwen's) task is understood as being broadly administrative; she is viewed as an assessor and allocated time accordingly. Whereas for the lecturer concerned her role is far more than that and involves a pedagogic engagement with learners and refuses the arbitrary separation of assessment from learning. To accommodate her sense of professionalism she works more intensively with students than her allocated hours permit. This is what James and Diment have in mind by underground learning.

> [Gwen] mediates and mitigates the effects of the official separation of learning and assessment by taking learning 'underground'. However this is a difficult option and she bears the cost of doing so (emotional as well as material) by herself. (2003, p. 418)

Such experiences are not unusual and reflect 'strains' within the sector. In Ainley and Bailey's study a lecturer commented:

> I have never worked so hard in my life and as long hours in a day, so many days in a week and I can't see it getting any better and I find that quite intolerable in some respects because I don't see how it's going to be possible to put boundaries around the expectation because of the drive for productivity. (1997b, p. 67)

A parallel can be drawn with work on primary schools. Menter *et al.* (1997) found that primary schoolteachers who sought to meet excessive administrative requirements, whilst at the same time seeking to deliver what they considered to be a valuable learning experience, were exhausted. Woods and Jeffrey (2002) examined the impact of this upon teacher identity and notions of professionalism. Their teachers became more alienated and restricted elements of former professional selves to their private lives, creating a context in which vocationalism was undermined. In the past teaching and professional identity was an all-consuming aspect of their lives but this had been replaced by a more instrumental approach.

How can we understand these changes? It is easy to draw upon the vernacular of proletarianization, deskilling and so on. For example, Randle and Brady, on the basis of a survey of college lecturers, assert:

> The deprofessionalisation of the lecturer is the outcome of government strategy. In order to significantly expand FE, whilst simultaneously reducing unit costs, it has been necessary to intensify work and this has been reflected in the struggle over new contracts. (1997b, p. 237)

And,

> The deprofessionalisation process in FE not only contains recognisable elements in the degradation of work but also represents a systematic de-skilling of the lecturer through the following:
> - displacement of teacher contact time by the beginnings of IT-driven flexible learning
> - loss of control over student management
> - lowering academic standards
> - assessment of performance by external agencies
> - prescriptive nature of, for example, GNVQ courses
> - a loss of control over intellectual property incorporated in new contracts. (1997b, p. 236)

These authors base their argument, in part, on the conflict between a professional and managerial paradigm as well as on the impact of new right education policy that celebrates the market and managers' right to manage (Randle and Brady, 1997b, p. 232). In a similar vein Hodkinson (1997) suggests that a post-Fordist rhetoric that embodies notions of learner centredness glosses over the neo-Fordist work relations present within FE that Randle and Brady, along with many others, have described.

Randle and Brady (1997a, b) have focused on processes of proletarianization and the loss of professional control that lecturers encounter. Drawing upon Derber (1983) they describe processes of ideological and technical proletarianization. Lecturers have lost ideological control over the purpose and goals towards which their labour is put as well as losing technical control over the labour process. This analysis suggests that lecturers currently experience far closer surveillance of their work than was formerly the case and that spaces for autonomy have become severely circumscribed. This literature raises a number of now familiar themes:

- loss of control
- intensification of labour
- increased administration
- perceived marginalization of teaching

- stress on measurable performance indicators. (Avis, 1999, p. 251)

For Gleeson and Shain these processes are more equivocal and rest alongside those involved with reprofessionalization. Whilst lecturers' work is being transformed particular aspects of professionalism become closed off whereas others are opened up. Gleeson and Shain identify three orientations adopted towards the conditions in which FE professionals are placed: unwilling compliance, willing compliance and strategic compliance (Gleeson and Shain, 1999; Shain and Gleeson, 1999). Such orientations straddle institutional positions and can encompass principals, middle managers and rank-and-file lecturers. Strategic compliers work with the progressive possibilities that change opens up and are characterized by a form of pragmatism which accepts some aspects of the new conditions as non-negotiable whilst others can be worked on progressively. These orientations can be mapped on to those explored by Alexandiou (2001), with the responsive and proactive manager bearing a similarity to unwilling and strategic compliance, whilst the entrepreneurial aligns with willing compliance. In some respects strategic compliers manage the relation between market realism and post-Fordist relations, working on the 'good side' of the latter. However, Gleeson and Shain's notion of a preferred professionalism that heralds progressive possibilities is undermined in several ways. It is set within a terrain in which FE managers have 'won' the right to manage (Gleeson and Shain, 1999; Shain and Gleeson, 1999). It is also circumscribed by fiscal concerns in which localized contextual issues about funding limit possibilities (see Kingston, 2004).

The conditions in which lecturers labour set the terrain in which they develop professional identities as well as accompanying notions of what it is to be a good teacher. In much of the work that has addressed these issues there is a tendency to homogenize lecturer experience whilst recognizing simultaneously that this is mediated by institutional and localized organizational cultures. Simkins and Lumby (2002) argue the importance of recognizing complexity and the varied conditions in which lecturers are placed. They for example have argued that clear-cut demarcations between managers and lecturers are often overstated, pointing out that for at least some principals:

> The self-perceived thrust of the cultural change attempted by many principals is to eradicate what is seen as the false dichotomy between a focus on management and a focus on teaching and learning, to shift to a perception that Janus-like, activities which apparently focus on different directions, actually both support students' total experience of learning. (Simkins and Lumby, 2002, pp. 16–17; and see Lumby and Tomlinson, 2000)

Lumby and colleagues imply, on the basis of their empirical work, that the slogan 'learners lie at the heart of what we do' is not without substance. However, those located within different positions in FE will favour particular and possibly contradictory strategies to pursue this particular end. Their claim is unsurprising and keys directly into the discursive constitution of the sector but it also clouds many of the contradictions and struggles present. The interests of the learner can rest readily with college mission statements and the allusion of a cross-college consensus as well as the presence of a common value system. To the extent that such a consensus exists it is of such a generalized form as to be ultimately meaningless, given the culturally diverse nature of further education. More importantly however, the learner and their interests are a powerful legitimating resource that can be marshalled rhetorically and discursively to support the interests of management as well as particular policy interventions. Professional capture has never been restricted solely to the rank and file.

Carole Leathwood's (2005) work usefully points towards the complexity present in the sector and similarly challenges a homogenizing view of the lecturer. She reminds us that lecturers' professional and work-based identities are not merely an adjunct of vocational cultures and responses to the conditions in which they labour, but that pivotally lecturers' class, gender and ethnicity is constitutive of their professional identity. She also infers that these processes are aged and sexualized.

> A number of lecturers [female] felt that senior management saw them as 'dinosaurs', who were unwilling to embrace the 'new' FE, with one saying that they were seen as 'nostalgic old women' ...
> Overt resistance led to the label of 'trouble-maker' ...
> The constructions of these lecturers' professional identities are not gender-neutral: deskilled, undervalued, not respected, feeling they should keep quiet and accept their lot. (2005, p. 398)

Leathwood similarly points to a connection between a caring orientation towards students that is in part constituted through gender as well as the way lecturers' classed and racialized identities are used as a resource to construct models of good teaching.

> Others drew on their individual and collective classed and racialised identities, as well as their identities as women, to construct themselves as 'good teachers' able to understand where students are coming from. (2005, p. 401)

Similar processes were discerned by Avis and Bathmaker (2006) in a study on male teachers new to FE, whose class informed their developing teaching and professional identities. For example, one of their respondents (Matt) drew on his experience of disadvantage and class origins, seeing this as offering an opportunity to connect with students drawn from a similar background. For other respondents class-based identities were also marshalled to connect with students, albeit that these identities derived from different class positions. Those who had held managerial positions drew upon this as a resource in both their relations with students and in their construction of professional and work-based identities.

New relations

It is clear that for many of those working within further
education as main grade lecturers the experience is less than
satisfying. The dichotomies that have been used to explore
these relations are somewhat limited in scope and reflect issues
around the following:

• professionalism	managerialism
• post-Fordism	neo-Fordism
• knowledge/subject specialists	facilitators of learning
• public service	market relations
• teaching	learning.

Early work such as that of Randle and Brady (1997a, b)
examined the lived experience of teachers recognizing that
teaching is a labour process akin to any other and is similarly
subject to the constraints surrounding waged work within a
capitalist society. This insight is by no means new and was
forefronted throughout the Thatcher years. Latterly it has been
reflected in New Labour's appropriation of the discourse of
effectiveness, efficiency and value for money (see Lawn, 1996;
Ozga and Lawn, 1981). This remains only part of the picture.
We also need to recognize the way in which arguments about
the nature of knowledge, teaching and learning feed into the
discussion of teachers' work. Here again we meet with contradictions and tensions. Elitist educational forms are set against
the more popular and inclusive. Social inclusion as a means of
generating social cohesion and the sorts of educational excellence suitable for the twenty-first century are a cluster of ideas
frequently expressed within government policy. Such policies
seek to take on board economic contingencies and value for
money. In a number of respects the issues are similar to those
examined in 'The strange fate of progressive education' (Avis,
1991a). In that paper I explored the way in which elements of
progressivism were appropriated and subverted by a vocationalism organized around capitalist interest. Such a process has
continued apace but what we are faced with in the current

conjuncture is a heightened emphasis upon upskilling and an understanding of the economic pay-off of a good general education (see for example Jamieson, 1993, pp. 200–1). These ideas sit alongside critiques of the narrowness of National Vocational Qualifications and, by some, the celebration of key skills (see for example Hodgson and Spours, 1997; Hyland, 1994).

Teaching relations

Emphasis is placed upon the individual learner with the teacher's role being to facilitate learning. Such a stress carries with it the shifts discussed earlier concerning teamwork and the facilitation of learning. The teacher is to become an expert facilitator of learning and therefore should be able to access and use a range of learning resources and techniques ranging from those derived from classroom practice to the use of information communication technologies (ICT). Therefore the teacher will have:

> the skills to plan and organise learning and the effective use of resources and learning technology (DfEE, 2001b, p. 3)

and be able to:

> Offer a range of flexible opportunities for learning including learning facilitated through information learning technology (Further Education National Training Organisation (FENTO), 1999, B3)

Unsurprisingly these themes are expressed in the Lifelong Learning UK (LLUK) standards that are to replace those of Further Education National Training Organisation (FENTO):

> Select and develop a range of effective resources to support learning.
> Use up to date technological resources and e-learning appropriately, and evaluate the success of these in enhancing the learning experience for learners. (LLUK, 2006, DP 5.1, DP 5.2)

Whereby it is anticipated that:

> our pupils are achieving higher standards than ever before, supported by a wide range of teachers and other adults, and by world-class ICT giving them direct access to world-class teachers. (Morris, 2001, p. 14)

Embedded within these processes is not only a model of the preferred teacher, but also a view of what constitutes good practice, both of which can readily fold back into a technicist construction of teaching. Performance management enables the state and its institutional arm within management to direct practice. Paradoxically, these technicist tendencies can be seen in the emphasis placed upon research (see Avis, 2001, 2002; Bloomer and James, 2001). Teachers are enjoined to engage in a process of:

> Reflecting upon and evaluating one's own performance and planning future practice ...
> engage in continuing professional development ...
> engage in research and study related to professional development (FENTO, 1999, unnumbered, G, G3a, G3c)

These themes are taken up in the current LLUK standards whereby teachers are to:

> Reflect on and demonstrate commitment to improvement of own teaching skills through regular evaluation and use of feedback.
> Evaluate own practice in relation to the promotion of equality, diversity and inclusive learning.
> Engage in further professional development activities drawing on and/or participating in research to enhance own practice, as appropriate. (LLUK, 2006, AP 5.1, AP 5.2, AP 6.1)

In particular there is the celebration of evidence-informed practice that is oriented towards the development of 'best' practice.

> We are now seeing more teaching that is based on clear evidence of what works. *We need to know that best practice is being identified, prized*

and mainstreamed as a matter of course. [My emphasis] (Morris, 2001, p. 26)

Teachers are to draw on research findings and use them to shape their own practice (MacLure, 2004; Oakley, 2000, 2002). However, the best practice model presupposes that research can generate such models. The use, for example, of literature reviews that examine existing research and draw from it pedagogic models of 'what works' to be generalized throughout the education system is fraught with difficulties. In the case of performativity and the redefinition of teacher professionalism the 'preferred' teacher is to be aware of such research findings and enact them within their own practice, to do otherwise would be construed as less than professional. Those who oppose such a redefinition of teacher professionalism are construed as cynics or as a manifestation of the 'forces of conservatism' – the self-serving professional (Avis, 2000). They are to be accorded no credibility and have no place in a modernized education profession. In a discussion of trust and professionalism Morris, the then secretary of state for education, commented:

> We need to challenge the cynics who argue that reform is impossible; that nothing can ever change; that the challenges are too great. These arguments have dogged the public sector for too long. No matter how well intentioned some opposition to reform may have been, it has sometimes ended up damaging the cause it was intended to serve. In education it is those who offer cynicism in the guise of experience who can drive young teachers to look for other careers. We shall always try to combat cynicism wherever it threatens progress on standards. (Morris, 2001, p. 9)

Such a standpoint sits closely with a management style that talks of tough choices and can easily turn into disciplinary practices which police those who question and challenge New Labour orthodoxies.

> Head teachers will often be faced with tough decisions ...
> They will also continue to face instances where they conclude that

they need to dismiss a teacher who cannot be brought up to the standards of the job. (Morris, 2001, p. 25)

What then is considered a valuable and valid educational experience? Here we confront the following notions:

- learner centredness
- relevance
- key skills:
  - communication
  - numeracy
  - problem solving
  - information technology
  - teamwork.

Subject or disciplinary knowledge is thought to be best acquired through a learning process marked by the above features. The process of learning becomes paramount. Learners are to be engaged. Teaching within such a context becomes reshaped and focused, moving away from a banking concept of education towards one in which there is a rhetorical celebration of learner empowerment (Freire, 1985). For many educationalists such ideas are unproblematic and can readily be set against the assumed sterility of traditional teaching (see for example, Edwards *et al.*, 1997). Who would seriously question learner engagement? The issue then becomes one of creating educational structures and curricular frameworks that can deliver such positive experiences. This concern has been expressed in many ways, in the work of Young and others on curriculum reorganization and in the call for a unified post-16 qualification structure (Finegold *et al.*, 1990; Hodgson and Spours, 1997; Young, 1998a). It is also reflected in the work of David Robertson who sought to encourage greater modularity or unitization of curricula in order to facilitate greater learner choice and flexibility (Robertson, 1994; and see Further Education Unit (FEU), 1992). Similarly quality systems and self-assessment regimes seek to shape arrangements that facilitate curricular reform (Further Education

Funding Council (FEFC), 1997a, b). Notions of accountability, performance indicators and systems of appraisal all figure in this process. This leads to the development of a constellation of ideas that help to shape a common sense of pedagogic relations. This common sense is shaped through the bringing together of a series of ideas and constituencies.

The new right introduced market disciplines and, importantly for the Labour Party, encouraged the development of a 'new realism'. Similarly understandings of globalization given a post-Fordist spin feed into this common sense, as do notions of good educational practice. We could talk about the formation of a social bloc allied to the development of an education settlement. The notions of social bloc and settlement are rooted in Gramscian Marxism and are important as they embody elements of compromise and fragility. Writing on Thatcherism Stuart Hall discusses the notion of a social bloc:

> The whole project of Thatcherism as a form of politics has been to construct a new social bloc, and in this project ideology is critical. A social bloc is, by definition, not homogeneous. It does not consist of one whole class or even part of one class. It has to be constructed out of groups which are very different in terms of their material interests and social positions. The question is, can these differences of position and interests be constructed into a 'unity'? (It never is a unity, in the strict sense.) Can these diverse identities be welded together into a 'collective will'? (Hall, 1988, p. 262)

The suggestion that there is an emerging education settlement which can hold together the interests of a range of constituents is important. The interests of learners, parents, educationalists, industrialists and the public at large are addressed by this settlement, with each constituent group having its concerns addressed (see Avis, 1993, 1998; Avis *et al.*, 1996). How this arises will vary. For example it will be claimed that an inclusive society and education system will reduce criminality by offering all a stake in society. In addition it will also offer learners not only skills relating to employment but also to life in general. Clearly there are contradictions and tensions within this settlement that are managed through negotiation and compromise. Such processes sit alongside the development of a social bloc, one that is understood as a type of alliance able to pursue its own interests. Again contradictions are paramount and are similarly managed.

When thinking about post-compulsory education and the formation of a common sense of teaching and learning we can see the embryonic development of such a social bloc, one that acts in tandem to secure its interests whilst presenting these as universal. This rests alongside a 'power' politics. I am reminded of those old Marxist ideas where bourgeois interests were represented as universal. Henry's comments, cited earlier in the chapter, could be understood through this lens and run nicely with currents in management theory that focus on vision, leadership, and tough choices (Holmes, 1993).

Within the various takes on the learning society, globalization and the need for inclusivity one can discern a transformation of the relations of post-compulsory teaching and learning. The drive is towards learner control of the pedagogic process with teachers being constituted as facilitators (and see DfES, 2006). This should not be understood as a totally homogenizing process as there are various positions that can be adopted. However, this move is set within the context of a hegemonic ideational framework which is so taken for granted that it is unquestioned and resolves the potential conflict between the needs of learners, communities and industrialists. This resolution is located within an acceptance of the all perva-siveness of market and capitalist relations. It can be seen in the realism of New Labour as well as in the writings of intellectuals who seek to move beyond the dichotomy of left and right, or who are trying to come to terms with the apparent collapse of socialism (see Giddens, 1994).

At this juncture it is useful to return to a more focused consideration of pedagogic relations. Self-assessment allied to performance management is a quality tool devised to encourage institutions to become committed to continuous improvement. It aims in the case of further education to encourage colleges to closely monitor their activities between inspections. It is assumed that by being involved in self-assessment colleges and course teams will be able to develop strategies of continuous improvement. As a result of the increased transparency surrounding for example teaching and learning, the course team and others would be in a position to detail the strengths and weaknesses of the current provision and thereby develop strategic planning. Within this practice we are witnessing the ongoing transformation of teacher professionalism – the licensed autonomy of the classroom teacher embedded in the *ethic of legitimated professionalism* has been disrupted and replaced by one of greater visibility (Grace, 1987, p. 208). The seeds of such change derive from the growth of managerialism within education and the welfare state, rooted in notions of quality and human resource management. However the gap between this and at least some forms of professionalism can be overstated.

> There are strong parallels with the traditional rhetoric/discourse of professionalism as a form of control, and similar tensions. HRM [Human Resource Management] harnesses the occupational/organizational culture to the delivery of efficiency and quality. Mutuality ensures commitment which produces increased economic effectiveness and development. The tensions between individualism and teamwork always prevalent in professional work are apparently resolved by the strong corporate culture, which creates a cohesive workforce but avoids workforce solidarity. (Menter *et al.*, 1997, pp. 65–6)

Gone is the isolated classroom teacher, in its stead there is a move towards a more 'collegiate' stance emphasizing teamwork. Within human resource management there is similarly a recognition of the importance of the team with culture seen as a vehicle of continuous improvement. A team that is held together through a shared vision is one which it is assumed will be able to deliver quality, in much the same way as a collegiate group of professionals will be able to deliver a good service. It is within this framework that one can understand the preoccupation with mission statements, as these embody both vision and commitment generated through the development of a shared culture.

The scope for mavericks is reduced and with it the space for teacher autonomy within the classroom, being replaced by the notion of the 'team player'. Self-assessment rests neatly alongside the new managerialism that introduces greater visibility, transparency and therefore control (Clarke and Newman, 1997; Clarke *et al.*, 1994). It works on a terrain that has largely been set by others. Rustin commenting on New Labour's project:

> The Blair project is that unless Britain can reach the standard of performance of its global competitors, in virtually every aspect of life, there is no hope of achieving lasting improvements in well-being.
> (Rustin, 1997, p. 7)

Within this framework we can understand the attempt to modernize and increase the effectiveness of institutions – transparency and visibility become vehicles of such a project. Self-assessment rests with other interventions in post-compulsory education and with these serves to facilitate the development of a regime of truth.

> Each society has its regime of truth, its general politics of truth: that is, the types of discourses which it accepts and makes function as true; the mechanisms and instances which enable one to distinguish true and false statements, the means by which each is sanctioned; the techniques and procedures accorded value in the acquisition of truth; the status of those who are charged with saying what counts as true.
> (Foucault, 1980, p. 131)

At its best self-assessment will lie alongside the settlement surrounding teaching and learning within post-compulsory education and will be validated by the material interests of the social bloc that supports the new settlement. It will rest with the common sense surrounding teaching and learning and be validated by the cultural ideas, vision and good practice of course teams. Lawn (1988, 1996) reminds us of the controlling nature of teamwork. Some years ago whilst discussing the changing definitions of teaching in primary schools he commented:

To be a good teacher, however, is not reducible to the technical knowledge skills described earlier [isolated, classroom based]. Throughout *Good Teachers* other qualities are outlined. There is a strong reference to the qualities a teacher must have – curiosity, sense of purpose, calm attitude, character, reliability and punctuality. One of these qualities, 'cooperativeness', is vital to the new role of the teacher in the team – developing school discipline policies, agreeing whole school policy and so on. So strong are these references to teacher qualities that they cease to be ideal characteristics of the good teacher and become part of a job specification for that teacher. To appear to have these qualities is in itself a new skill requirement of teaching. Without appearing to be cooperative, there will be no secure job. The definition of the teacher has subtly altered – no longer the classroom generalist, they will be part of the team, a professional team; for professionalism is here defined as a collective matter in teaching. (1988, p. 166)

Such a description that moves towards a more collegiate stance is also present within human resource management and the development of quality systems. Such collegiality, as with the new managerialism, rests upon a model of teamwork operating within conditions set by others. For example, the course team who develop their own mission statement in line with their institution, but whose team members will be evaluated by criteria set elsewhere. Here we meet with Hargreaves' notion of contrived collegiality from which, in the current climate, there seems little escape (Hargreaves, 1994, pp. 195–6).

Managerialism

Work on the labour process of lecturers following incorporation in 1993, which carried moves towards market and competitive relations, has often been portrayed as encouraging masculinist and bullying styles of management (see Kerfoot and Whitehead, 2000; Leonard, 2000). More recent work has suggested that overtly bullying and masculinist forms of management within further education colleges have been to some extent tempered. Deem *et al.* (2000) would in part attribute this process to the emerging feminization of management within the sector as well as with the departure of the first wave of post-incorporation management (see also Cole, 2000; Hughes, 2000). Gleeson and Shain (1999) from a rather different position would point to emerging cooperative and collaborative relations developing within the sector that hold the excesses of marketization in check (Shain and Gleeson, 1999). Drawing upon the work of Seddon (1997), they suggest that at least some senior managers are striving towards a form of preferred profession-alism that opens up progressive possibilities marked by more collaborative relations, both within and across institutions. Such directions are also reflected within the state in the move away from institutional competition towards an emphasis upon collaboration and partnership (see for example DfEE, 1998c). Within this context performance management can be portrayed as a more appropriate and nuanced mechanism to direct institutional practice when set against market compe-tition. In this way performance management has become incorporated within taken for granted institutional practices. This can be seen in internal processes of self-assessment and in directives from the regional Learning Skill Councils through which institutional targets, goals and performance indicators will be developed. Such practices serve to distance managers and the rank and file from the arbitrariness of management diktat. In this instance performativity becomes embodied in a regime of truth that refuses other conceptualizations of good practice which become silenced and are denied legitimacy. However despite these strictures performance management, with its panoply of targets and performance indicators, has now come to be deemed by many, including some former supporters, to have reached its limits and to have become a rather blunt instrument. For example, Hargreaves writes:

> Government-by-target is widely accepted to have reached its limits as a strategy. Targets are still an essential part of the toolkit, but setting linear improvement goals and then pushing hard to achieve them can no longer be the dominant principle for reforming large, partly autonomous organisations. (2003, p. 9)

And Chapman (2002) from a health perspective, which he suggests is just as applicable to education, claims that centrally determined targets of anything but the most general kind are antithetical to improvement (and see Hargreaves, A., 2003; Sachs, 2003a, b; Stronach *et al.*, 2002). Colleges, like hospitals, are complex systems and the imposition of centrally determined targets can lead to a series of unintended consequences, not least amongst which is the loss of morale and autonomy. Gleeson and Shain's work illustrates the way strategic compliance serves to wrest progressive possibilities from the conditions in which FE is placed. Strategic compliers work with the progressive possibilities that change opens up and are characterized by a form of pragmatism that accepts some aspects of the new conditions as non-negotiable, whilst others can be worked on progressively (see Seddon, 1997). Inter- and intra-college collaboration is a means by which lecturers attempt to regain some control over their labour process and mitigate the intensification of work through sharing course materials and so on (see Gleeson and Shain, 1999; Shain and Gleeson, 1999).

Revitalized teacher professionalism

A number of writers have called for a revitalized teacher professionalism. Some of these writers have commented upon the uniqueness of FE and the way in which its workforce is fractured and diversified as a result of the varied vocational cultures from which lecturers are drawn. Although these cultures are seen as pivotal to lecturer identity, they are also vulnerable because of their perishability. This is because the claim to having recent and relevant work experience inevitably erodes over time (Gleeson and Mardle, 1980; Robson, 2002). The fractured professionalism characteristic of FE lecturers renders this a weak bulwark against the inroads of managerialism and performativity. In response Robson has argued the different vocational cultures present within FE colleges could in a sense be reconciled through the development of a professionalism oriented towards pedagogy and practice (Robson, 2002; Viskovic and Robson, 2001). Robson, for example, calls for the development of a distinctive FE professionalism that would be able to challenge the banalities of management practice whilst also contributing towards the development of pedagogy. Hodkinson holds a somewhat similar position and calls for a revitalized teacher professionalism that draws upon a post-Fordist rhetoric:

> So the rhetoric goes, if schools and colleges are continually to improve quality whilst cutting costs, in an ever changing educational c ontext post-Fordist solutions are essential. These would entail for example:
> i. giving teachers more responsibility for their own work, both individually and as members of teams;
> ii. giving those teachers regular access to high quality training;
> iii. giving the core teacher workforce greater financial rewards and greater job security in reward for greater flexibility;
> iv. minimising the divide between teachers and school managers, such as heads and deputy heads; and
> v. running schools as collaborative teams. (1997, p. 73)

There is an echo here of Hargreaves' discussion of teaching for the post modern age in which 'The rules of the world are changing. It is time for the rules of teaching and teachers' work to change with them' (Hargreaves, 1994, p. 262).

Guile and Lucas (1999) argue that earlier models of teacher professionalism within further education organized around subject specialisms have been undermined. Along with other writers they call for an expanded professionalism, organized around the notion of the learning professional. They call for a model of professionalism that shifts from one based upon insular towards connective knowledge. They align this with five shifts:

1. subject knowledge to curriculum knowledge
2. teacher-centred to learner-centred pedagogic knowledge
3. intra-professional knowledge to inter-professional knowledge
4. classroom knowledge to organizational knowledge

5. insular to organizational knowledge (derived from Guile and Lucas, 1999, pp. 216–17)

There is an affinity between these shifts and conceptualizations of reflexive modernity as well as with the emphasis that has been placed upon mode 2 knowledge in such conditions. For Guile and Lucas the concept of the FE teacher as a learning professional:

> denotes the need for an active engagement with those economic, educational and technological changes which have brought about new professional responsibilities and have profoundly altered the context of professional activity. (1999, pp. 217–18)

The efficacy of such a strategy depends upon the way in which we make sense of wider social structures. If we conceive of education as a site of struggle, as located within a society that is characterized by capitalist relations which spawn structural inequality and antagonistic relations, we would require a politics that moves beyond particular institutional arrangement to a wider societal engagement.

Gleeson *et al.* (2005) push the notion of the learning professional to its furthest and as with others they take on the notion of an expanded professionalism and place this alongside Stronach *et al.*'s (2002) call for a restorying of professionalism. For Gleeson *et al.* the challenge is to develop a transformative model of professionalism located within a community of practice that is based upon reflexive solidarity. In this understanding professionalism moves towards an engagement with civic society, becoming rooted within forms of participatory democracy. The work of Ranson (2003) and others is drawn upon to support this argument. There are echoes here of Habermas and the attempt to form a speech community based upon rational and therefore democratic decision making. Such a model utilizes a notion of an expansive professionalism that is committed to social justice.

The conditions of reflexive modernization related to uncertainty and risk provide the material base on which to develop a progressive professionalism. This can be glimpsed in Ranson and Stewart's discussion of learning democracy in which the resolution of manufactured uncertainty arises through the development of a democratic politics based upon civic engagement and related to Habermassian critical theory (1998, p. 260). Professional relations based upon performativity are seriously flawed and in response there has been a call for the development of a form of professionalism based upon a deliberative politics marked by dialogue and negotiation across a range of constituents who have an interest in educational processes. This is reflected in the work of many writers; Codd, for example calls for:

> The restoration of trust, I suggest, presupposes a form of professional accountability in which the moral agency of the professional is fully acknowledged ...
>
> In this form of accountability, the professional practitioner has the moral obligation to render an account to several different constituencies, which may have different or conflicting interests. This will involve judgement and sometimes the resolution of an ethical dilemma through a process of reflection or deliberation. This may be a collective process, shared with one's professional peers ... (1999, p. 52)

The work of Nixon *et al.* moves towards a deliberative process calling for a dialogic politics that recognizes difference and incommensurable interests and which views deliberation as a way of resolving potential conflict (Nixon, 2001; Nixon and Ranson, 1997; Nixon *et al.*, 2001). In this argument the claim to professional expertise is given less salience. However, despite the undoubted sophistication and complexity of these arguments there is a tendency to veer towards a consensual if not pluralistic model of the social formation, one in which differing interests and incommensurable difference can be harmonized through dialogue (Mouffe, 1998, p. 13). Consequently, whilst recognizing difference and incommensurability, they are tied to Habermassian conceptions of rationality and reason. Habermassian critical theory associates dialogue with an ideal speech community in which power has no place as it distorts the democratic relations that enable reasoned dialogue. Although these ideal conditions are aspirational they are nevertheless undermined by the relation between discourse and power as well as by the forms of social antagonism present in the social formation, key amongst which is that between capital and labour. These difficulties can be overcome by a professionalism that is expansive and open to the wider society. Such a professionalism seeks to engage in dialogue but recognizes the forms of antagonism present in society and attempts to resolve difficulties by drawing upon an ethical commitment to social justice. This commitment recognizes that not all differences can be harmonized through dialogue. If we take seriously reflexive modernization and the radical uncertainty that surrounds this, a democratic and dialogic form of professionalism would seem appropriate.

Conclusion

That we are witnessing the increasing proletarianization, deskilling and intensification of labour within further education catches the lived experience of many who work within the sector. We can see quite clearly such processes reflected in increased teaching loads and in the transformation of the nature of teaching and learning. However this is only part of the picture and sits alongside attempts to modernize teaching and learning. Such attempts aim to transform the social relations of work and to close off, or at least play down, some of those activities previously central to teacher identity and sense of worth. This could be described as a process of reprofessionalization, but here again the terms fail to grasp the unevenness and contradictoriness of processes involved.

Running alongside the increased surveillance of teachers' work lies a genuine interest in improving teaching and learning. A number of colleges are seeking to embed a research culture that can contribute towards continuous improvement.[1] However these interests are located within a modernizing strategy that seeks to increase the value addedness of educational processes and thereby the competitiveness of the economy. We are witnessing the ongoing transformation of what it is to be a college lecturer. Terms such as proletarianization and reprofessionalization approximate but ultimately fail to fully grasp these processes. Proletarianization captures the concerns with financial rectitude as well as the interest in shaping teacher identity so as to form and align these with models of good practice. Such models are built into self-assessment regimes forming part of the construction of the good teacher. It is against such models that the individual will be measured and course teams assessed, with teaching observation and self-assessment being the strategies employed. Yet simultaneously the interest in effective pedagogy opens up a space for teachers to seize and utilize to develop new forms of expertise. Here again the context of reprofessionalization is problematic, being set in conditions that are determined by others. It may be banal to reiterate but deskilling, upskilling and reskilling occur concurrently within professional work and provide the site of struggle. What is certain is that the labour process is being transformed and with this new identities and stakes are being generated over the construction of what it is to be a lecturer. Michael Apple (1996), whilst discussing the new right, draws our attention not only to the oppressive nature of these ideas but also to their 'good sense'. There are progressive possibilities within the new conditions and relations of teaching and learning embodied in moves towards dialogic, reflexive and related models of praxis. However these possibilities are constrained by the discursive context and forms of surveillance in which they are embedded. These constraints are incorporated in New Labour's consensual politics that operates within a capitalist hegemony and provides both the stake and site of struggle. The worry is that the language of rights, social justice and inclusion become appropriated by a reformist capitalism and turned back on themselves becoming subordinated to a capitalist logic. This logic rests upon an easy consensus that denies social antagonism and thereby is able to appropriate the language of rights, social justice and inclusion for its own interests whilst apparently universalizing these. The educational task is to ensure that it does not occur.

The development of expansive learning communities that link practitioners to wider social movements, together with the restoration of relations of trust in educational institutions, would herald progressive possibilities. However, these possibilities are constrained in all sorts of ways. Within further education the lived realities of working in the sector seem to preclude such practices for many. The move towards light-touch inspections for those deemed successful can in part be seen as a restoration of trust, one able to encourage innovatory practice that could benefit learners. Yet this move beyond performativity is limited, being based on a conditional trust predicated upon sustained performance (Avis, 2003). Earned autonomy is located within a context that accepts and works within current state strictures – the acceptance of the competitive education settlement and all that goes with it (Avis, 2003).

Yet arguments that herald a new professionalism provide a resource that can be drawn on in struggles over the educational labour process, as well as wider social conflicts. The rethinking of accountability would be a case in point, whereby it becomes part of deliberative processes located in civil society deriving sustenance from a commitment to social justice as well as a recognition of social antagonism (Gleeson *et al.*, 2005; Ranson, 2003). It is well to remember that the hegemony of capitalist relations has to be continually resecured and the rhetoric and materiality of the knowledge economy is the latest version of this.

Note

1 See for example Unwin's (1997) discussion of the development of an MA research-based course located within a college; see also Solihull College Research Policy (undated); and Elliott (1996b).

6

Knowledge, curriculum and power

This chapter draws upon earlier analyses exploring the construction of knowledge and curriculum in PCET, seeking to relate these to issues of power. It engages with discussions of socially situated learning and the manner in which this articulates to the production of knowledge. It explores different conceptualizations of the curriculum 'as fact' and 'as practice' and examines the orientations of public educators and industrial trainers towards knowledge. This analysis is set against a social realist model of knowledge that offers a caveat to processual and situated understandings of the curriculum. The chapter concludes by exploring the limits and possibilities of curricular frameworks within which post-compulsory education is placed. The chapter anticipates subsequent arguments developed in the following chapter that call for an expansive notion of practice which extends beyond the classroom.

Education in general and post-compulsory education in particular is charged within the competitive settlement to deliver learners who can contribute to and enhance the effectiveness of the economy by developing forms of human and intellectual capital that align with the needs of industry. Regardless of the level or type of curriculum encountered the learner is to acquire the skills and dispositions required by the economy. Whilst such aspirations are both unobtainable and socially divisive they nevertheless inform educational policy and the curriculum that learners encounter. These aspirations are unobtainable because of the diversity of capital and, as Rikowski (2001) has argued, it is unable to specify its needs. In addition these aspirations are socially divisive in as much as learners are placed within a social and occupational structure marked by iterative patterns of inequality.

There is a paradox surrounding the context within which post-compulsory education and its curriculum is placed, deriving from the tension between ideas concerning the knowledge economy and the intrinsic characteristics of capitalism. The former notion has an affinity with analyses that stress the participatory processes of learning and which also view the workplace as a site of learning as well as of knowledge production. Such participatory ideas have a progressive, if not radical veneer, carrying a dialogic and learner-centred model of pedagogic relations – providing a learning context in which learners together with their teachers 'produce' knowledge. The paradox is that these notions can just as easily sit with a deeply conservative modernizing agenda as with a more progressive one. Arguments that emphasize the socially situatedness of workplace knowledge, its specificity and located 'use value' can readily fold into forms of knowledge that secure the interests of capital as against those of human empowerment. Within debates that address work-based learning there is a tendency to view some workplaces as offering pedagogic opportunities and others as not (Fuller and Unwin, 2003). Unsurprisingly, the result is that those workplaces seeking to develop the skills of the workforce are seen to offer learning opportunities. These, however, will be set on a very particular terrain that aligns at best with a modernizing agenda and construes employer and employee interests as being in harmony or at least minimally compatible and certainly not antagonistic. There is an affinity between this argument and those that suggest the nature of capitalism has been transformed whereby the skills and knowledge of the worker have become pivotal to competitive advantage and consequently older antagonistic relations have been superseded.

Current theorizations of the curriculum and learning

emphasize the socially situated nature of both as well as allied processes of knowledge production. Such ideas are present in work that has addressed teaching and learning within further education as well as that which has examined worked-based learning (Garrick and Rhodes, 2000; JVET 2003; and see Chapters 3 and 4). These analyses suggest learning occurs as a result of social participation within a community of practice. As against Lave and Wenger (1991) and Brown *et al.* (1989), writers such as Fuller *et al.* (2005) and Avis *et al.* (2002) construe the classroom as in some ways analogous to work-based communities of practice. Through social participation within a community of practice variously located at work or within education, learning may take place with the resulting changes to learner identity.

Learning leads to the transformation of identity and can be construed as a social process through which the individual changes and becomes a different person. This is because learning can be seen as a process of becoming and as one of identity formation and transformation. Indeed Biesta (2004) describes learning, drawing upon Derrida, as a form of transcendental violence. At the same time, through participation within a learning community, whether in PCET or at work, knowledge is produced and not simply received. This is not to ignore the social contexts in which learning takes place, or indeed the patterns of exclusions that surround such processes which marginalize or exclude. The earlier arguments view the curriculum and learning as a social and constructed process. Such insights are not dissimilar to those developed by the new sociology of education in the 1970s that operated with a constructivist model of the curriculum but also drew attention to its arbitrariness and imbrications with power (Young, 1971, 1977, 1998a, b, 1999; Young and Whitty, 1977). The latter points, although acknowledged in more recent accounts, tend to be sidelined, with these analyses stressing the activity of learning and teaching and paying less attention to curriculum deconstruction. If the curriculum is construed as being socially constructed this is accomplished in the classroom or learning context that is inevitably at one stage removed from the formal curriculum, as indeed it is from wider structural relations present within the social formation.

Michael Young (1977) some years ago made a distinction between the curriculum as practice and the curriculum as fact (and see Young 1998a). The curriculum as practice is in part reflected in those accounts that emphasize the participatory nature of learning. It considers the process of learning and is somewhat agnostic in relation to its substantive content. The argument is that it is the values that underpin pedagogic processes which are crucial rather than the particular form of knowledge encountered (Moore, 2006). There is an echo here of Raymond Williams' (1973) notion of the public educator, as well as the position of other radical and progressive educationalists who sought to construct pedagogic encounters that were meaningful to those who had been marginalized and excluded from education. Such writers called for dialogic, learner-centred, democratic and participatory pedagogic processes. These positions whilst seeking to offer meaningful and relevant educational encounters also acknowledged the arbitrary nature of the curriculum as well as its ties to the status quo and relations of power (see for example Apple and Buras, 2006).

Bourdieu recognizing the arbitrary nature of the curriculum suggests there is nothing intrinsically unique about the knowledge incorporated as against that which is excluded (Bourdieu and Passeron, 1977). To reiterate, it is in this sense that there is nothing that separates the knowledge embodied in the curriculum from that which is excluded. Although the curriculum is in this sense arbitrary, it is nevertheless tied to class and other interests. There is a homology between elite and high-status curricular forms and privileged groups within society. It is partly because of this that such groups are able to reproduce their privileged positions from one generation to the next. This is particularly the case for the middle class, many of whom can only trade on their symbolic and human capital to reproduce their privileged positions. Bourdieu's conceptualizations of cultural capital and habitus are important as they point towards the way in which class advantage can be carried into and resecured through educational processes (Bourdieu and Passeron, 1977; and see Chapter 4).

The argument that the curriculum embodies the interests of those with power within society is by no means new and has been a long-standing feature of radical critiques (Young, 1971). Michael Apple (1979; Apple and Buras, 2006), for example, has frequently drawn attention to the way in which classed, gendered and raced interests are present within the curriculum. Crucially, he qualifies this association by pointing out that these curricular interests are also struggled against, often in complex and contradictory ways, by those who are excluded. When considering curricular debates and the relationship between these and classed, raced and gendered interests it is important to distance the analysis from a determinist standpoint. Such a strategy enables the recognition of a number of important features: the complexity of the processes encountered, the contradictions that are embodied within the curriculum, the spaces provided for appropriation by subordinated groups, as well as the ongoing historical development of the curriculum itself.

Earlier I referred to the work of Raymond Williams, making a connection between his notion of the public educator and other radical and progressive currents. Such ideas can be readily appropriated, albeit in contradictory ways, by curriculum and conservative modernizers (see Avis, 1991a). This is particularly appropriate in the new conditions facing post-compulsory education where the rhetoric surrounding economic change calls for the knowledgeable and creative worker who is able to operate successfully in the uncertainties of the present. Despite the dangers of curricular appropriations by conservative currents, it is nevertheless important to recognize insights derived from a processual view of the curriculum. This position sees the curriculum as accomplished through classroom processes and subject to a series of mediations by teachers and learners. It is this very indeterminacy that offers a space for struggle as well as for outcomes that are contrary to those of policy makers and curriculum designers. Yet, it is also important to recognize the wider structural relations within which the curriculum is located, that are related to the operation of power and class interests in society. It is quite possible for progressive, if not radical, curricular relations to be accomplished within the classroom as part of a dialogue between learners and teachers, but for this to be set within an ongoing pattern of social relations that serves to reproduce classed, raced and gendered inequalities. Examples of this process can be seen in the experiences of learners following access to higher education courses (Warmington, 2003), or within adult education provision (Crowther *et al.*, 2005), or indeed amongst business studies students in full-time further education (Avis, 1991b). One way of recognizing such complexity is to consider various levels of analysis, ranging from classroom relations through to institutional relations and the way in which these are located within regional, national and global contexts. At each level there will be different politics and scope for struggle that carry with them varying limits and possibilities.

Some years ago Denis Gleeson described the tripartite structure of further education.

Tertiary modern	The 'new' FE; incorporating the unqualified, unemployed and unemployable. Curricular emphasis is on generic skills via remedial vocational education, 'voc prep', work experience and 'social and life skills'.
Craft	Mainly day release craft tradition (male dominated); but now incorporating female craft skills: hairdressing, beauty therapy, catering, nursing and so forth. Curricular emphasis is on training for home and non-work.
Academic-technical	Full- and part-time academic/technical tradition incorporating the concept of 'educated' skilled labour. Here the curricular emphasis is on 'education' via English, mathematics and science.

(Gleeson, 1983, p. 38)

Although the above was written more than 20 years ago the divisions that Gleeson points to remain in place, an echo of which was present in the Dearing Report (1996). In 1995 Sir Ron Dearing was invited, by the then Conservative secretary of state for education, to consider and advise on the ways in which the framework for 16–19 qualifications could be strengthened. The subsequent report proposed a national framework of awards for 16–19-year-olds in which there were four levels[1] and three pathways, aiming to introduce a level of coherence and clarity to the qualification structure. The three pathways were the academic (GCSE and A level), applied education (GNVQ) and vocational training (NVQ). Parity of esteem was expected, as was a degree of mobility between pathways.

> I recommend that the distinguishing characteristics appropriate to each pathway should reflect the underlying purpose, as outlined below.
>
> **A Level and GCSE**
> - where the primary purpose is to develop knowledge, understanding and skills associated with a subject or discipline
>
> **Applied education (GNVQ)**
> - where the primary purpose is to develop and apply knowledge, understanding and skills relevant to broad areas of employment
>
> **Vocational training (NVQ)**
> - where the primary purpose is to develop and recognise mastery of a trade or profession at the relevant level (Dearing, 1996, pp. 15–16)

The interests of the then Conservative government were reflected in the pathways indicating their desire to retain the 'gold standard' of A levels. Nevertheless the report, by proposing a national framework for qualifications and holding out the possibility of modularity with students working across a number of pathways, offered the potential for more radical curricula. Writers such as Michael Young, Ken Spours and others responded to the Dearing Report seeking to further its radical and progressive potential (Hodgson and Spours, 1997;

Young and Spours, 1997). Some years earlier Young (1993), drawing on research on the British baccalaureate, argued in favour of inter-disciplinarity, the integration of the vocational with the academic and the development of a curriculum marked by connectivity (Finegold *et al.*, 1990; and see Young, 1998a).

In a reprise of earlier debates the Tomlinson (2004) committee was established by New Labour to consider the structure of the 14–19 curriculum, and reported in 2004. Many commentators had hoped that the report would presage a thoroughgoing reform of the curriculum as well as the quali-fication framework in directions anticipated by the British baccalaureate. Although this proved to be the case, with the report echoing many of the features of the British baccalau-reate, New Labour failed to break free of the dominance of A levels and, as with its Conservative predecessors, remained wedded to this qualification. However, as a result of Curriculum 2000, A levels were split into A/S level and A2s. At the same time the 14–19 strategy introduced vocational pathways for those young people with vocational interests, a number of whom would have been disaffected from or disillusioned by the traditional school curriculum (and see Hodgson and Spours, 1999 for discussion). The tripartite divisions within further education to which Gleeson referred, whilst subject to cosmetic changes, remain firmly in place, being linked to processes of class formation and the ongoing reproduction of inequality.

In some respects Gleeson's tripartite structure corresponds to the distinctions made by Williams, i.e., those of the industrial trainer, public educator and old humanist. However, in current conditions these are being reworked to accord with different economic circumstances. Jamieson in a discussion of vocation-alism argued that:

> Fundamental changes in the economic infrastructure and the structure of occupations have forced increasing parallels to be drawn between vocational education and liberal education or, to use more conventional terms education and training. In essence the argument

is straightforward. It is claimed that we have seen the passing, at least in the advanced industrial world, of the sort of semi-permanent occupations which require an easily identifiable set of skills for which training could be designed and given. In the 'post-industrial' world, citizens and workers are required to master an ever widening range of complex information. What is needed it is claimed, is the ability independently to acquire new knowledge and skill, so that learning how to learn becomes increasingly important. People also need to understand the procedural nature of work, to improve their problem solving skills and to be able to move flexibly from one task to another as the situation demands. (1993, pp. 200–1)

One of the ways in which we could think about these changes is the impact they have had upon the orientations of industrial trainers. This orientation is concerned with meeting and addressing the skills required in work and encouraging young people to develop the forms of disposition and orientation to work as well as the skills needed in waged labour. Jamieson implies that these requirements have become both more generic and less rigid. They are no longer tied, as they once were, to the specific requirements of a particular occupation. In some respects there is an affinity between this type of argument and hegemonic understandings of the economy, which instrumentalize and economize all education, whereby at its most basic it is to serve the needs of the economy. Education becomes necessary to develop the generic skills required by the economy, as against the specific skills required by particular occupations.

There is a homology between the arguments of industrial trainers and curriculum modernizers, as well as currents within progressive education. The orientation of industrial trainers to education and knowledge was one in which the learners would be inducted into the knowledge and skills that they required at work. It is as if the curriculum is external to these young people's practice, something to be acquired rather than developed through work-based activity. I am reminded of Michael Young's (1998a) description of the 'curriculum as fact' and of Freire's (1985) 'banking concept' of education. Although these notions have been applied to the traditional and academic curriculum, they nevertheless convey an important feature of the orientation of industrial trainers. This orientation when taken to its extreme becomes embodied in competency-based training, a model that has been resoundingly critiqued by Hyland (1994) for its reductionism and anti-educational conse- quences. However, in current conditions processual models of teaching and learning have assumed a prominent position.

A contemporary version of the industrial trainer is reflected within the concerns of curriculum modernizers who would call for an updated curriculum that is fit for the twenty-first century. A processual model of the curriculum, marked by participatory relations within which teachers and learners actively produce knowledge, would sit well with the interests of curriculum modernizers. This is because through such a curriculum learners would develop the forms of adaptation, flexibility and disposition that are allegedly required by twenty-first-century capitalism. Leadbeater echoes these senti- ments when he suggests the radical innovation that underpins economic growth thrives in dissenting culture where authority is constantly challenged (Leadbeater, 1999, p. ix). The point is that the interests of industrial trainers and curriculum modernizers as well as those calling for a processual under- standing of curricular relations can come together in an uneasy alliance. This alliance is contradictory, messy and points in a number of different directions simultaneously but nevertheless secures, or at least is not antithetical to, the interest of capital. What I have in mind is that whilst critique and creativity is valued, as is the notion that knowledge is not merely received in pedagogic encounters but is actively produced within this curriculum framework, these practices can nevertheless easily fold over in the direction of conservative interests. This is because such practices are set on a terrain centred upon capitalist interests embedded in the competitiveness settlement and is one that forms the taken for granted backdrop to these pedagogic and curricular relations. Without a clearly politicized understanding of curricular relations and of the contextual location of post-compulsory education, it is relatively easy for apparently progressive and radical positions to be appropriated by hegemonic and conservative interests (see Avis, 1991a; Fielding 1988).

The foregoing discussion should not be read as validating the 'curriculum as fact'. This curriculum model aligns with that of Williams' 'old humanists' who saw education as a conversation with the past where the learner is introduced to the body of knowledge present within society, that is to say knowledge that is socially prescribed, which is deemed to be external and that is to be 'mastered' by the learner (Young, 1977). Thus, for example, within literature the student would be introduced to the canon of English literature, Shakespeare, Chaucer and so forth. Although this curriculum will have been socially constructed it is presented as a body of knowledge that the learner is to appropriate and reproduce.

Much has been written about the exclusions that are embodied in this the received academic curriculum. It has been castigated for its arbitrariness as well as for being centred upon a particular 'ideal' student (Keddie, 1971), one who is white, academically able and middle class. The academic curriculum, exemplified within A levels, has been castigated for its class basis as well as its sterility and lack of engagement with wider society. It has also been criticized for its lack of connection and relevance to the current socio-economic context in which education is placed. It has therefore been subject to the critiques of both curriculum modernizers and other radical currents. There are two points that need to be made. First, although the academic curriculum is a received curriculum and can readily sit with a 'banking concept', this can be overstated and certainly plays down the possibilities for dialogic forms of pedagogic practice within the classroom (see Bloomer, 1997). However, we need to recognize that the assessment structure of academic subjects may place an undue emphasis upon regurgitation and thereby construe the curriculum as fact to be memorized. This is reflected in the A level examination structure, and especially in the distinction between AS and A2s. Second, it is undoubtedly the case that social interests inform and shape the curriculum, whereby classed, gendered and raced interests become embodied within it. Yet academic knowledge forms may at the same time offer a vantage point from which to view and critique wider society.

The received curriculum cannot be reduced solely to the play of class and other interests, as within it there may be forms of knowledge and conceptualization that could be bent to serve the interests of the oppressed and disadvantaged. In other words the way in which the curriculum is accomplished within the classroom may well be contradictory. On one level it may correspond to and secure the interests of the middle class, on another it may provide an intellectual resource that could be appropriated by progressive social movements to challenge patterns of inequality. It could then become a resource to be used in the struggle for social justice. In addition the academic curriculum, in social democratic fashion, offers a route to status-enhancing knowledge and therefore provides access to mobility as well as positions of power, albeit for a minority of learners. There is an inherent danger with this position in that it can easily fold back into the myth of meritocracy. However, Paul Warmington's (2003) work on Access courses illustrates the way in which students wished to utilize the knowledge and skills they had developed in the course of their studies in order to give something back to their communities. Such an orientation is by no means unknown and is also a feature of professional work whereby professionals who enter education wish to give something back to their occupational community (see for example Avis and Bathmaker, 2006).

The curriculum 'as fact' or 'as practice' is a convenient descriptive device, though both offer rather crude models, the former is often construed as aligning with conservative and elitist interests, whilst the latter is thought to rest with progressive and radical interests. We need to be attentive to the accomplishment of the curriculum within the classroom and to the forms of knowledge that are validated, as well as the social relations that are present. In other words it is important to interrogate the politics of classroom relations and to examine the ways in which these can interrupt, support or have an equivocal relation with the structures of power present within society. Such an analysis can point towards the limits and possibilities for radical action within and outside classroom practice.

The traditional academic curriculum of Williams' 'old humanists' is often wrongly construed as embodying 'truth' and 'certainty'. This is why Young describes this curriculum 'as fact' as it is accorded a spurious objectivity that rests outside history and thereby denies its own historical formation. One of the insights derived from the *Transforming Learning Cultures project* is the emphasis given to participatory processes present in pedagogic relations as well as the way in which learning transforms identity (see Chapter 4 and JVET, 2003). Such an analysis can point towards the way in which the academic curriculum reproduces classed, gendered and raced privilege through the formation of a particular type of middle-class subjectivity and identity, one that is, by virtue of its formation, more accessible to those drawn from privileged backgrounds.

The notion that the academic curriculum exists outside time and space, having an objectivity validated by its knowledge claims rather than through the power of social groups to assert their interests, is fallacious. This conceptualization of the objectivity of the curriculum derives from a particular historical period during which this notion of the curriculum carried a special weight. This was the moment when mass schooling developed and was also a time when social movements such as the trade unions and feminist groups in the late nineteenth century and early to mid-twentieth century struggled to ensure their constituents had access to high-status knowledge (Shilling, 1988).

Bernstein captures the idea of the curriculum 'as fact' in his description of 'socialisation into knowledge is socialisation into order' and that 'educational knowledge is impermeable' (1977, p. 98). He sets this concrete experience of the curriculum against the recognition of the ultimate mystery of the subject, which he describes as one of incoherence:

> The ultimate mystery of the subject [discipline] is revealed very late in the educational life. By the ultimate mystery of the subject, I mean its potential for creating new realities. It is also the case,

and this is important, that the ultimate mystery of the subject is not coherence, but incoherence: not order but disorder, not the known but the unknown. As this mystery ... is revealed very late in the educational life ... only the few experience in their bones the notion that knowledge is permeable, that its orderings are provisional, that the dialectic of knowledge is closure and openness. *For the many, socialisation into knowledge is socialisation into order, the existing order, into the experience that the world's educational knowledge is impermeable.* [My emphasis] (1977, pp. 97–8)

There are two points to be made. First, whilst the curriculum can be experienced as one of fact it is nevertheless socially produced and its certainties are often illusionary. The second point draws on the discussion of work-based learning in Chapter 3, as well as the way in which social and economic relations are currently understood. We meet with well-rehearsed arguments that describe the risk society, conditions of reflexive modernization and the requirement for the knowledgeable worker. These arguments coincide with a notion of the rapidity of change – a 'runaway world' (Giddens, 2002) in which innovation is endemic and where the certainties of knowledge become increasingly untenable. The recognition of such uncertainty and the problematic nature of knowledge is no longer restricted to an elite, but has become generalized throughout the society. For Giddens (1998) and Beck (1999) this development offers democratic possibilities as the claims of experts are no longer held in awe. Experts within the same field frequently disagree on the appropriate course of action. We have only to reflect on the debate about global warming as but one example. In such an ideational context knowledge claims become permeable. It is at this juncture that mode 2 knowledge becomes increasingly important, not so much for its validity but rather for its use value – its contribution to 'what works'. This process sits alongside the economizing and instrumentalizing of education. Educational processes become valued for what they contribute towards economic well-being, that is to say rendering the society competitive in a global marketplace.

The problematization of knowledge linked with a concern with what works aligns with what Beck and Young (2005) describe as genericism, a term derived from Bernstein. In this case subject-based knowledge is no longer validated by disciplinary conventions but rather through its contribution to the economy. For Beck and Young genericism creates a new kind of knowledge structure, one that is:

> linked explicitly to the perceived demands of employers and to their assertion that future employees would need to become more 'flexible'; and they [generic modes] assumed that becoming more 'flexible' was a demand that was common to a wide range of occupations, tasks and jobs. (2005, p. 190)

This move aligns with reflexive modernization and the subsequent blurring of boundaries between different academic disciplines as well as with the development of broader learner skills, all of which sit comfortably with the move towards genericism.

The argument in this chapter may seem far removed from the immediacies of practice, having said little about curricular engagement. It is here that the work of Young, Lacey, and Brown and Lauder is useful, as is the cluster of terms they have used to examine curricular issues. Lacey, and Brown and Lauder marshal terms such as 'collective intelligence' that refuse an atomized model of the learner, replacing this with a collective subject, one who seeks solutions to the problems of our time and therefore moves beyond existing practice.

> Collective intelligence [is] defined as a measure of our ability to face up to problems that confront us collectively and to develop collective solutions. (Lacey, 1988, pp. 93–4)

> Collective intelligence can be defined as empowerment through the development and pooling of intelligence to attain common goals or resolve common problems. It is inspired by a spirit of co-operation (Brown and Lauder, 2000, p. 234)

Similarly, Young's notion of 'connectivity' recognizes the significance of interdisciplinarity and the arbitrariness of curriculum divisions.

> In the sense used here, connective specialisation is concerned with the links between combinations of knowledge and skills in the curriculum and wider democratic and social goals. At the individual level it refers to the need for an understanding of the social, cultural, political and economic implications of any knowledge or skill in its context, and how, through such a concept of education, an individual can learn both specific skills and knowledge and the capacity to take initiatives, whatever their specific occupation or position ...
>
> As a curriculum concept it points to the interdependence of the content, processes and organisation. As a definition of educational purpose it aims to transcend the traditional dichotomy of the 'educated person' and the 'competent employee' which define the purpose of the two tracks of the divided curriculum. (Young 1993, p. 218)

Such an orientation towards knowledge has, as with the notion of collective intelligence, the potential to pose new solutions to the socio-economic difficulties we face. These understandings recognize the social, cultural and historical processes that lie behind the curriculum. They also acknowledge the arbitrariness of this, as well as recognizing the nexus of power that shapes the curriculum. Notions of 'critical intelligence' and 'connectivity' bear some relation to mode 2 knowledge and serve to challenge traditional academic and disciplinary divisions. These approaches prioritize the process of knowledge production as well as its specificity by linking the production of knowledge to situated learning. These forms of intervention hold progressive possibilities, albeit that these are not inevitable and are the outcome of struggle.

These forms of engagement need to be linked to the wider social structure and pattern of power, for without this connection they can easily be appropriated by a neo-liberalism or a modernizing agenda – after all constant innovation is a feature of capitalist society. The development of 'critical intelligence' and 'connectivity' together with localized and situated engagement may produce new knowledge that can be readily appropriated and bent to capitalist interests. Connectivity and mode 2 knowledge have been located within post-Fordist models of the economy, one characterized by constant innovation as well as the endless requirement for new knowledge that can be marshalled for product development, whether this is in the service or manufacturing sector.

The issue for progressive and radical educators becomes the manner in which processual models of the curriculum can become linked to a wider politics that recognizes social antagonism but also seeks to develop really useful knowledge. Part of such a strategy would aim to go beyond localized conditions by making links to wider structural relations present within society and would also seek to draw on existing forms of knowledge that have use value. It is at this juncture that Young's social realist model of knowledge is helpful in as much as he argues that such knowledge cannot be simply reduced to class interests and ideology but has value that extends beyond this. I am reminded of Althusser's (1969) discussion of scientific knowledge and theoretical practice in which he argues that this practice, whilst in the last instance determined by the economy, has its own level of determinacy and relative autonomy. In this way knowledge will have its own value and use, having its validity assessed by criteria applicable to scientific and theoretical practice.

For Young's social realist model the objectivity of knowledge rests upon the practices and conventions of the disciplinary community from which it derives – a community that is socially and historically located. This conceptualization links mode 1 and mode 2 knowledge in as much as it questions a crude understanding of the curriculum as fact and connects to mode 2 knowledge as it anticipates a situated form of knowledge that derives from a particular community of practice. The validity of such knowledge is determined by the accepted conventions of that particular community. The danger here, as with Althusser's prescriptions, is one of idealism and that of 'normal science'. That is to say the community of practice becomes wedded to a particular disciplinary model, one embodying particular social interests and characterized by a specific discursive 'truth' (Geras, 1977). Although as Young recognizes, within a particular disciplinary community of practice there will be contestations concerned with what counts as knowledge as well as its nature. He writes:

> Bourdieu offers us an approach to theory/policy relations by reminding us that seeing intellectual fields as sites of power struggles is not incompatible with having a commitment to truth and objective knowledge. (2004, p. 18)

These ideas drawn from Bourdieu serve to locate and in a sense qualify the way in which Beck and Young utilize a social realist understanding of knowledge. Notwithstanding the equivocations that surround such knowledge they argue it carries epistemic gains which are not immediately accessible to other forms of knowledge. This allows such knowledge to be appropriated and to become really useful knowledge for oppressed groups, to be marshalled in the struggle for social justice.

In his early work Young (1977) recognized that we need to move beyond the duality of the curriculum as fact or as practice. One way in which this can be accomplished is to value the insights derived from each position. The curriculum as practice points towards the situated and participatory processes through which knowledge can be produced, but as such faces two difficulties. First, that of relativism, whereby it becomes tied to the specific and localized context in which it is developed, becoming merely an interpretation that has no wider validity beyond that particular context. It can easily become a parody of itself validating what learners know but failing to move beyond that point, as was the case with some forms of progressive education in the past (Jones, 1983; Sharp and Green, 1975). It becomes a conservative practice as it fails to challenge or move learners beyond their existing starting points. The second danger surrounding the curriculum as practice is that it can easily slip into a genericism that seeks unreflexively to meet employer requirements and so in turn becomes a form of conservative practice. The curriculum as fact carries the danger of being elitist and exclusionary. Yet at the same time there may be spaces within it for those marginalized by education to develop and acquire really useful knowledge that could be used in the struggle for social justice. This potential derives from the epistemic gains that such knowledge may offer.

Curricular and pedagogic engagements need to offer, in Biesta's (2004) terms, the potential for 'transcendental violence'. Dialogic forms of curricular practice that enable learners to carry everyday knowledge into the classroom and set this against disciplinary/academic forms provide the possibility that the learner may interrogate these and develop understanding. There is nothing particularly radical about this argument and it aligns with what many teachers already do in the classroom. A more radical stance is introduced if classroom relations are set not only alongside wider structural relations but also against patterns of social antagonisms that exist within society. Such an understanding acknowledges the relationship between knowledge and social interest, albeit that the former is not overdetermined by the latter, retaining its own level of autonomy. This suggests that learners and teachers need to interrogate the curriculum for the social interests it embodies as well as for its progressive possibilities. This interrogation would include not just the formal curriculum but also the way in which it is enacted or lived in the classroom and would recognize the contradictions and tensions this involves.

Such an engagement with the curriculum and classroom practice would move towards a politicized understanding, recognizing social antagonism and the difficulties posed at this specific point in time. That is to say a conjunctural moment in which the competitiveness settlement is hegemonic, constituting an unquestioned common sense for which managerialism and perfomativity provide important ideological bulwarks. The classroom and pedagogic relations provide a space in which critical and radical understandings of the social formation can be developed. But in themselves such insights derived from within the learning context are easily undermined, being amenable to co-optation by a modernizing capital. The radicalism of approaches that concentrate overly on learning and teaching practices are undermined, often stopping at the classroom or college door.

We need to think about the manner in which curricular practices can engage with the wider society and particularly those progressive currents and social movements concerned with social justice. There is a need to move beyond the college or indeed the workplace as a learning site. Neary's (2005) notion of an academic activism offers such a possibility, and although this is oriented towards the university some of its elements are applicable to PCET and further education. Neary suggests that academic radicalism 'owes much to popular and critical pedagogy, [it differs] in that the focus of activity for academic activism is the academy' (Neary, 2005, p. 8). Whilst such a position seems counter to my earlier argument this activism calls for academics to engage in politicized struggles against the inroads of managerialism and perfomativity. Such struggles connect with an interest in wider conflicts that lie outside of the university and with a concern to offer students the opportunity to develop 'really useful knowledge' that can be marshalled in the struggle for social justice. Academic activism is part of a radical praxis that seeks to link the university to wider social struggles. Such a model would be as appropriate for PCET as for the university.

Aronowitz (2006) in a similar manner offers a way of linking processes within education to those outside. He argues that the experience of performativity and managerialism as well as the loss of autonomy and spaces for academic freedom within the academy constitute sites of struggle that can only be addressed by collective organization and action. Aronowitz suggests that such struggles and resistance against subordination and control can readily link with anti-oppressive struggles which arise outside the academy. The experience of working within US universities, whilst at one stage removed from PCET in the UK, resonates with the lived experience of those labouring in the sector and points to the way in which connections can be made to wider societal structures and conflicts. Aronowitz claims that the experience of 'subalternity' within the academy, and in this case further education, can resonate with the experience of other subaltern groups, not only in the local and national context, but also globally.

There is a difficulty with the preceding argument as it can be portrayed as hopelessly naive and utopian. At least two points need to be made. The attempt to make education conform to the needs of capital has intensified in recent years as a result of the rhetorical flourishes that surround globalization and the call for competitiveness. Such intensification generates its own sets of contradictions, tensions and indeed spaces in which alternative understandings can be struggled for. Capitalism whilst endlessly innovative is at one and the same time destructive and constantly creates tensions and difficulties which generate opposition. Neither capital nor the state and its agents can ever completely control what goes on in the classroom. Indeed the very notion of these categories, particularly that of the state and its agents, may be less than helpful. Capital encompasses a range of different forms and is not homogeneous. The state and its agents, however defined, will be marked by contradictions and therefore will contain the possibility for progressive appropriation. Within the state there will be currents that are antithetical to capitalist interests, and indeed may have an ambivalent and uneven relation to capital, albeit that these relations may be under the sway of a hegemonic formation that argues 'there is no alternative' to globalization and capitalism.

Although we may recognize the difficulties faced by education for the development of radical practice the notion of radical democracy may be helpful. This notion suggests there is an ongoing struggle for democracy and that as one set of antagonisms are overcome new ones arise. Radical democracy is an aspirational politics that may not be fully achieved but one which operates with an expansive notion of social justice. The task in hand is to think about the way in which such notions could be embedded in curricular relations. The following chapter addresses more directly the question of practice, arguing for an expansive model that is embedded within a notion of social justice.

Note

1 Dearing's four levels

National Award: Advanced Level

AS and A	GNVQ	NVQ
Level	Advanced level	Level
3		

National Award: Intermediate Level

GCSE	GNVQ	NVQ
Grades A–C	Intermediate Level	Level
2		

National Award: Foundation Level

GCSE	GNVQ	NVQ
Grades D–G	Foundation Level	Level
1		

National Award: Entry Level
common to all pathways
three grades A/B/C

Source: Dearing, 1996, p. 13.

7
Social justice, post-compulsory education and practice

Current trends in educational theory and state concerns with educational research have placed a premium upon interventions into practice. These developments are inherently messy, facing in both conservative and progressive directions simultaneously. The latter is thought to offer a politics of hope as well as the possibility of subversion of existing relations. Interventions into educational practices may provide opportunities to undermine patterns of disadvantage associated with class, race and gender that have been ongoingly reproduced through educational processes. It is at this point that an interest in social justice can be located, one not so far removed from the traditional concerns of social democracy. Indeed social democratic approaches often acknowledge the structural contexts in which learners are located and view these as amenable to policy interventions. English policy developments such as Sure Start (Whitmarsh, 2005) or Education Action Zones (Gewirtz et al., 2005) could readily rest within such a framework. This is what New Labour has in mind when it calls for joined-up thinking. Such interests have a long history.

This chapter explores a potential tension between an interest in social justice and the ongoing improvement of practice. To address this I initially examine two rather different types of literature. First, two early policy documents that address post-compulsory education and, second, I touch upon current debates concerned with educational research. The linkage between these two sections is that both bodies of literatures have an interest in the development of and changes to educational practice. In addition part of this literature has been criticized for its location within a technical or instrumental rationality that paradoxically runs counter to its aspirations to improve practice. Hodkinson *et al.* (1996) write:

> This term derives from the work of Habermas (1972), and is analysed further by Grundy (1987), Held (1980) and Gibson (1986). In essence:
> 'instrumental rationality represents the preoccupation with means in preference to *ends*. It is concerned with method and efficiency rather than with *purposes* ... It is the divorce of fact from value, and the preference, in that divorce, for fact.' Gibson (1986, p. 7).
> Such technical rationalism assumes that people can be managed as if they behave like machines. Education and training are seen as production, using the metaphor of the assembly line, with inputs, processes and outputs. Quality and efficiency dominate the discourse. (p. 120)

To begin, I want to draw briefly upon two key policy documents set in different historical contexts that are used to locate the discussion. These documents have been highlighted as significant by authors associated with the *Transforming Learning Cultures in Further Education* project (Colley *et al.*, 2005; Hodkinson, 2006). Specifically, I want to consider the Further Education Unit's (FEU) *A Basis for Choice* (1979) and the Audit Commission's *Unfinished Business* (1993). There are two reasons for doing this; one is to point towards an unsurprising continuity in the concern to improve practice within post-compulsory education. The second is that an examination of this work provides both a contextualization for, as well as a corrective to some of the current debates surrounding the sector. These debates seemingly imply that a move beyond the technical rationality and perfomativity embedded in managerialism offers progressive possibilities, in a fairly straightforward manner.

Another theme of this chapter focuses upon educational research and those critiques recently forwarded by the state and other commentators which suggest that this research has not engaged sufficiently with practice and therefore has failed to make any significant impact upon learning and teaching within the sector. These critiques lie behind the imperative that the interests of users are addressed in bids for research funding and that users should become involved in the evaluation of research – one example being the forthcoming Research Assessment Exercise of 2008. These critiques call for a re-emphasis on practice. They embody the hope that research can make a difference to teaching and learning in the sector and that it would thereby be able to contribute towards the improvement of practice leading to widening opportunities as well as the extension of social justice for learners.

The concluding sections of the chapter explore the notion of practice. I return to the *TLC project* and in addition consider the work of Lingard *et al.* (2003a, b). These sections seek to explore the notion of practice and set this alongside an expansive understanding that locates practice within its wider socio-economic context. Such a contextualization recognizes the structures of inequality present within society as well as the way in which social and economic measures can be thought of as aspects of educational policy.

A basis for choice and unfinished business

The FEU's[1] *A Basis for Choice* (*ABC*) was published in 1979, and was an educational response to the growth of youth unemployment in the 1970s as well as the development of youth training schemes by the Manpower Services Commission, a state quango. *ABC* was deeply critical of much that took place within further education and was concerned with provision for those young people who had few if any qualifications and who were unclear as to their vocational orientations. *ABC* sought to provide a pre-vocational curriculum framework for such young people, one that would be able to interest and motivate them.

Elsewhere I have developed a critique of *ABC* that construed it as an attempt to form types of subjectivity amongst young people that were in accord with the presumed needs of capital (Avis, 1983). Here I want to address *ABC*'s critique of traditional further education that it castigated for its elitism, lack of responsiveness and failure to address the needs of under-achieving young people. The elitism of further education was epitomized in its orientation to craft- and technician-based vocational education as well as its involvement with academically oriented Ordinary and Advanced level provision. Pedagogically the sector was construed as didactic, with much teaching seen as teacher centred and out of kilter with the needs of school underachievers. *ABC* readily sat with a form of progressive practice that aligned with social democratic interests. The aim was to create a pre-vocational and pedagogic context in which underachieving young people could develop broader skills as well as educational potential. This was to be achieved within a pedagogic context in which young people's emerging vocational interests were used to motivate them and rested alongside a common core that would enable learners to develop a range of key skills that would enhance problem-solving skills, teamwork and so on. In many respects there are continuities between the critique of FE mounted by *ABC* and subsequent interventions both pedagogically as well as in policy terms. This can be seen in the forms of pedagogy that are currently dominant in further education teacher training which adopt a similarly progressive stance (Harkin *et al.*, 2001). This is also reflected in the development of vocational pathways that in the same way seek to open up opportunities for disaffected school underachievers. *ABC* aimed, within its particular sphere, to intervene in FE practice and to transform teaching and learning. It sought to develop or enable the transformation of identities for learners and teachers, with the hope that the former would thus be empowered. Its intervention into educational practice had an aspirational aim to create a space for radical improvement – by this I have in mind the transformation of practice in progressive directions that serve to enhance the opportunities provided for young people. Thus far, and in some respects, I have provided an over-optimistic and one-sided account. My reason for doing this was to draw out the good sense of this intervention, but this was clearly compromised by its concern with what we would now describe as conservative modernization. *ABC* bought into conventional thinking that addressed the relationship between education and the labour market and not unsurprisingly failed to develop a critique of capitalist education. Yet within its own terms it sought to transform what it construed as elitist educational practice and to open up further education to a wider constituency of underachieving young people. It was firmly wedded to a social democratic understanding of social justice and aligned itself with progressive practices. These aimed to address the needs of learners and provided pedagogic encounters responsive to these, offering students relevant and potentially empowering educational experiences.

Fourteen years later the Audit Commission published *Unfinished Business* (1993). Phil Hodkinson (2006) has described this report as a key moment in the development of audit culture and managerialism within further education. He has also castigated it for its rootedness within a technical rationality that fails to comprehend the complexity of learning and teaching within post-compulsory education and training. Whilst the Audit report is centrally preoccupied with questions of measurement and value for money, being in this sense very much located within a crass and narrow perfomativity, it nevertheless simultaneously carries a critique of FE practice and complacency. In some respects the report resonates with *ABC* in its concern with learners' placement on particular courses and their subsequent retention, achievement and progression. *Unfinished Business* could be viewed through a leftist or social democratic reading, one interested in social justice and concerned with young people's placement on inappropriate courses. The Commission's solutions may have been crude and rooted in audit and technical rationality but did seek to intervene into practice, to call the sector to account, and thereby contributed towards some sort of notion of educational improvement.

Hodkinson and Bloomer (2001), along with others, have sought to question and debunk the attempt to measure educational outcomes in the way in which the Audit Commission proposed. They rightly argue that the complexity of educational processes and the life worlds in which young people are placed render such a project deeply flawed. The many case studies conducted by Bloomer and Hodkinson (1999) and other researchers provide ample evidence of the pivotal role that happenstance plays in retention, achievement and progression. The danger of this position is that we then neglect the structural and iterative patterns that surround educational processes and outcomes. The point is that we need to be wary of reading too much into micro or localized patterns. The very complexity of such relations may serve to cloud structural processes that are intimated at by patterns of retention, achievement and progression.

The salience of *ABC* and *Unfinished Business* is that both interventions sought to transform FE practice. Both reports, whilst written at different conjunctural moments, could be read through a social democratic lens. The Audit report, with its emphasis upon audit and accountability, rests comfortably with elements within New Labour, whereas *ABC* accords both with New Labour and a liberal progressivism. However, the apparent commitment of both reports to widening participation, the development of opportunities and erstwhile commitment to social justice are comprised through their rootedness within conservative modernization and capitalist hegemony.

Although the Audit Commission's report could be described as technically rational and thereby deeply flawed it does nevertheless share common interests with *ABC*. The reason for drawing upon these reports is that both ultimately attempted to transform practice in conservative directions. *ABC* sought to prepare young people for waged labour within a capitalist society whilst the Audit Commission sought to implement forms of accountability that secured managerialism. It is important to recognize that a technical rationality which draws upon audit and managerialism is but one approach that could be marshalled in the pursuit of conservative modernization. It is a strategy that can be drawn upon at appropriate moments to discipline and surveil workers, one related to the balance of force between labour and capital. Labour process theorists have long pointed out the varying strategies used to control and exploit workers, ranging from laissez-faire to tight managerialism. Audit, target setting and managerialism is but one such strategy. It is important to recognize that although these practices are currently wedded to policy making, the forms of target setting associated with audit have come to be seen as increasingly problematic by those who would in the past have supported them as tools of educational improvement (Hargreaves, 2003, p. 9, 26; Mulgan, 2004, p. 96). Bentley and Wilsdon write:

> The current preoccupation with setting national standards as a basis for accountability obscures a tension that the process of adaptive reform must address; the specification of performance standards often narrows the scope for organisational innovation. This is partly because it encourages risk aversion, but more importantly because it establishes rigid parameters of organisation and formal responsibility. (2003, p. 23)

These writers then judiciously add:

> This does not mean that targets and standards are not essential. But they must be used judiciously, and owned by the participants, rather than used primarily as an instrument of control. (p. 23)

Indeed David Hargreaves points towards the inadequacy of targets, and by default, models rooted within a technical rationality as a vehicle of enhancing practice:

> All levers have their limits ... Moreover, when a new lever has a demonstrable positive impact, policy-makers tend to push the lever beyond its potential. For example, in England 'targets' ... have had a real effect on raising standards, but when targets work policy-makers impose yet more of them. The danger, of course, is that this can induce resistance to the very notion of a target and thus ruin what was originally an effective lever. (2003, p. 22)

Approaches that recognize the complexity of educational processes would now be seen as more appropriate tools for the modernization and enhancement of practice within the sector, albeit that this is set within a capitalist hegemony.

Education research

Paradoxically, the preceding discussion mirrors those concerned with the relationship between educational research and the development of improved practice within the sector. There is the same tension between a notion of technical rationality and the recognition, by at least some writers, that such approaches deny the complexities surrounding educational practice. These writers would suggest that, whilst approaches rooted in forms of technical rationality appear to be concerned with the improvement of practice, they can easily fold into its antithesis. By failing to address the complexities of educational practice such approaches can easily negate their aspirations to improve practice and thereby forward social justice. It is argued that more nuanced accounts able to address the complexities and messiness surrounding educational processes are needed that will offer a greater contribution to the improvement of practice. These accounts will be better suited to address issues of social justice. There are a number of issues that need to be considered. First, how is practice understood in research that has sought to improve teaching and learning within post-compulsory education? Second, and relatedly, how are these processes made sense of in relation to a political economy of education that seeks to subvert exploitative and oppressive relations which are consistent features of capitalist society? In consideration of these themes it is useful to return to earlier debates that addressed the salience of educational research. Initially, I will touch upon Hammersley's contribution to the debate in the 1980s. This is followed by a brief examination of later debates that have attempted to tie educational research closely to the improvement of practice, as well as to a particular model of research rooted within a quasi-positivism aligned to a technical or instrumental rationality. The current interest in the use of systematic reviews for the enhancement of practice epitomizes this particular orientation to research and its underlying technical rationality.

In the late 1970s and early 1980s neo-Marxist analyses of educational processes occupied an important and influential place within the sociology of education. This work sought to explore the relationship between education and the reproduction of structures of domination with respect to class, race and gender. Paul Willis's (1977) work was seminal, and in relation to further education, a number of authors drew on approaches that could sit comfortably alongside such an analysis. However, it should be noted that some of this work took more seriously gendered processes and were accented towards an analysis of patriarchy and its relationship to class (Bates, 1990, 1991; Skeggs, 1988). These accounts in effect provided a political economy of education, and whilst learner resistance was explored there was no detailed discussion of practice within education (Avis, 1984, 1985; Bates, 1990, 1991; Skeggs, 1988, 1997). Sections that addressed 'what to do on Monday morning' were fairly cursory and gestural. The strength of such work was to emphasize processes of class reproduction as mediated by race and gender, and in this way pointed towards a political economy of education, that linked educational processes to the labour market. More recently papers by John Preston (2003) and Helen Colley (2006) provide examples of work that has returned to that tradition. Often such work is strong on analysis but appears relatively weak in terms of practice.

In the 1980s Martin Hammersley expressed his frustration with the quality of education research (1984, 1985, 1987), arguing much work within the sociology of education was located within a paradigmatic mentality. By this he meant work was often judged on the basis of its location within competing paradigms rather than on its quality. In other words he implied that research was evaluated on the basis of its politics rather than its intellectual rigour. In addition he argued that such research neglected to spell out its implications for practice and therefore failed to make an intervention into educational relations or indeed policy debate. These two inadequacies meant that the sociology of education was failing to develop as a discipline. A plethora of ethnographic accounts had been written but these failed to contribute towards either the cumulative or theoretical development of the discipline, and had only a slight relationship to the improvement of pedagogic practice or indeed the concerns of policy-makers. There is a resonance between this critique of educational research and those that were subsequently developed towards the end of the twentieth century and into the twenty-first.

In the following paragraphs I draw out three connections after which I return to the question of practice and the political economy of post-compulsory education and training. The first connection I want to make concerns the relationship between educational research and practice. Many would argue education is an applied discipline and that research should be centrally concerned with practice. If research does not address practice it should not rest within education and be located elsewhere (Elliott, 2001b; Pring, 2000). The second connection I want to make concerns the critique made of the rigour of research. Finally, there is a worry about the connection between practitioners and academic research. This leads into the use of practitioners to evaluate research on the one hand and on the other to a renewed interest in practitioners as researchers of their own practice.

For some time now the state has had a considerable interest in the improvement of educational practice through the application of research findings. Bodies associated with the state have encouraged the development of practice-based research or have drawn upon users to evaluate research findings. The Learning and Skills Development Agency, recently subsumed within the Quality Improvement Agency for Life Long Learning and Learning Skills Network, has supported and funded research that addresses this aim. A series of action research projects have been funded that, it is hoped, will have a direct impact upon teacher practice (see for example Cousins, 2002; Maynard and Smith, 2004; Mullins, 2005). This interest in the utilization of research to inform practice has been strongly supported by the state. The Learning and Skills Research Centre (LSRC) has been established, which also has an interest in research that enhances practice in the learning and skills sector (Morris, 2002). The EPPI-Centre (Evidence for Policy and Practice Information and Co-ordinating Centre) located at the Institute of Education in London has a remit to disseminate evidence-informed research as well as the production of systematic reviews. Similarly the Economic and Social Research Council, which funds the more prestigious research projects in the UK, is concerned that research findings address user needs and, in the case of educational research, contributes to the ongoing improvement of practice. Not unconnectedly, and along with others, Hodkinson (2004) argues that there is an attempt to put in place a new orthodoxy for educational research (and see Hammersley, 2005; Lather, 2003). This orthodoxy determines what counts as 'good' educational research and, one might add, ties educational research firmly to a commitment for the improvement of practice. Such interests have been reflected in the activities of the National Education Research Forum (see for example NERF, 2001) as well as in reviews of educational research conducted in the 1990s (see for example, Centre for Educational Research and Innovation, 2002; Hillage *et al.*, 1998; Tooley and Darby, 1998).

A more recent interest of policy-makers is in the use of systematic reviews to gather evidence that can be used to inform and improve pedagogic practice. The call for evidence-informed practice, systematic review and similarly oriented practitioner research is wedded to a particular conception of educational research embedded within the new orthodoxy. Such a conception is marked by technicization and instrumentalism, in as much as research is to address a particular problem, to conjure solutions or at least interventions, as well as meeting the rigorous standards of what is to count as educational research. These issues will be addressed in terms of their resonance with a quasi-positivism that is characteristic of the new orthodoxy. Later I return to the way in which these issues can sit alongside a view of practice that is not rooted in technical rationality but which has equally conservative ramifications.

The quasi-positivism of these approaches operates within a form of crypto-functionalism. It is assumed a consensus can be attained that can be used to direct educational practice. This crypto-functionalism implies that agreement can readily be attained about what constitutes good practice, as well as the evidential basis upon which such judgements are made. It is at this juncture that the technicization and instrumentalism of such approaches become conjoined. The consequence is that the social antagonisms within which educational relations are placed become sidelined, if not hidden from view. These processes could be thought of as attempting to construct a generally accepted common sense of what counts as educational research, as well as good if not best practice.

The state views the development of evidence-informed practice as an important vehicle that can be used to improve the effectiveness of educational practice, with systematic reviews leading to the dissemination of good, if not best practice (Avis, 2003). Despite claims to the contrary, these notions are rooted within a quasi-positivism (Davies, 2000; Gough, 2000; Oakley, 2000, 2002). Hammersley (2001), for example, argues that systematic review assumes the superiority of a positivist model of research. This is a result of the methodological criteria used to evaluate studies that place experiments, randomized controlled trials and statistical analyses at the top of a 'credibility hierarchy' (see Hammersley, 2001, pp. 544–5). This positivist tendency can be seen in the procedures underpinning the process of systematic review:

The principles which we attempted to work to were those outlined earlier for systematic reviews, viz:
- a clear specification of the research question to be addressed;
- systematic and exhausting searching for studies;
- clear criteria for including and excluding studies;

- assessments of methodological quality of studies;
- strategies to reduce bias in selection and reviewing; and
- transparency of the methodology for carrying out the review.

(Evans and Benefield, 2001, p. 533)

The tenor of this particular discourse is located within a specific understanding of research and implies that through this process unequivocal data can be produced. Systematic review, through its inclusion criteria as well as a rigorous assessment of the methodological quality of studies and a clear specification of research questions, will be able to assess the quality and implications for practice of existing research. In this way systematic review will produce evidence that can inform practice, call practitioners to account and offer a counter to the obfuscations of academics (see Oakley, 2000). The aspirations of systematic review are akin to what Latour describes as science:

> Science is certainty; research is uncertainty. Science is supposed to be cold, straight and detached; research is warm, involving and risky. Science puts an end to the vagaries of human disputes; research creates controversies. Science produces objectivity by escaping as much as possible from the shackles of ideology, passions and emotions; research feeds on all of those to render objects of inquiry familiar.
> (Latour, 1998, pp. 208–9, cited in Nowotny *et al.*, 2002 p. 2)

Systematic review, through the clarification of the research question and its concern with what works, seeks evidence that can inform good practice and pursues certainty (EPPI, 2001). Paradoxically, this scientific project has been tried before. Pring (2000) has discussed the way in which 'scientific' approaches to educational research conducted in the early years of the twentieth century aimed to produce generalizable data but failed in this aspiration (see Oakley, 2000 for discussion). This project foundered because of its conceptualization of research and the nature of the evidence produced. It sought through the use of rigorous methods to produce data that would have the status of fact and be able to inform practice. Such approaches failed because they were, and indeed are, unable to accommodate the complexity of classroom relations (see Elliott,

2001b; Thomas and Pring, 2004). Even in their own terms such approaches fail. Maclure (2004) argues that systematic review, with its stress upon tightly defined research questions and rigorous exclusion and inclusion criteria, often ends up with an extremely small number of primary studies. The result is that the claim that such reviews can inform practice is misleading and prone to error.

While the state has championed the development of what Hodkinson (2004) has described as the new orthodoxy of research, work located in this framework is problematic as it simplifies educational relationship, and to the extent that this is carried into processes of systematic review, these too suffer the same difficulties. This critique then suggests other more open and dialogic approaches to research and practice, and specifically those that move beyond the limitation of technical rationality have more to offer. They will be able to make a greater contribution to the improvement of practice and furtherance of social justice through a recognition of the complexity of educational relations. These analyses may then draw upon the involvement of practitioners in the research processes.

Thus far the orientation of research towards a technicized model of educational practice has been examined. In what follows I explore the way in which research has addressed teaching and learning within post-compulsory education. This work has sought to improve practice and in this section I discuss the way in which practice is understood, as well as the manner in which educational processes are made sense of in relation to a political economy of education.

Politics, practice and social justice

The preceding discussion raises a number of issues, two of which I will comment upon. First, it pointed towards a critique of technical rationality and the assumption that education research can provide easy answers to pedagogic issues. These discussions raised arguments that addressed the complexity of classroom relations. A second issue concerned socio-logical analyses of education, particularly those rooted within reproduction theory. Hammersley's (1984) discussion of the paradigmatic mentality was examined, as was the suggestion that such approaches, whilst strong in analysis and political positioning, were relatively weak in addressing practice. Gewirtz and Cribb (2003) echo this position when they argue that academic researchers should forgo the moral high ground and become more involved in practice. They describe this in terms of a shift in social scientific analyses, one that derives from the critique of post-structuralism, which encouraged the development of forms of social scientific analysis that moved away from those 'modelled upon *episteme* (analytical, scientific knowledge)' towards those 'based upon *phronesis* (practical judgement or wisdom)' (p. 247). In a separate paper Gewirtz (2004) refuses Hammersley's position on value freedom. In some respects these moves towards practice reflect the inade-quacies and dangers of theory as well as postmodern positions that refuse grand narratives and which therefore focus upon immediate and localized spheres of practice.

The ESRC's *TLC project* marshalled a similarly complex under-standing of learning and practice, one that constituted this as socially situated practice. Although this understanding of practice was located within an elaborate theorization, the very complexity of localized educational practices meant that these could or maybe should only be evaluated within the context in which they arose. As a result of this complexity there were in effect no general claims of substance that could be made or applied to improve classroom practice. Nevertheless, despite this emphasis upon learning as a socially situated activity, there was a recognition of the salience of the social structure in educational relations, albeit one mediated through learners' habitus as well as by the dispositions carried into educational settings. Hodkinson *et al.* write:

> Learning cultures are often persistent and many of the determining influences are outside of the control of players within the education system. However, because learning cultures are partly constructed

by people there is scope for some significant change through which improvements in learning can be brought about. Some of the improvements necessary in FE require wider issues of social inequality and restrictions of the labour market and employment practices to be addressed. (2005, p. 8)

As a result of the complexity of pedagogic relations the structural context has in a sense been bracketed. This standpoint in part derives from a theoretical position that seeks to acknowledge agency whilst at the same time refusing determinism. This position also in part derives from the requirements of this ESRC-funded project that was concerned with pedagogic questions leading the authors to concentrate 'on the potential for change inside FE' (Hodkinson *et al.*, 2005, p. 8). These contextual issues have an impact upon the way in which practice is conceived. There is a link here with the earlier criticism of educational research, particularly that which criticized the sociology of education for its neglect of practice, as well as for its tendency to lean towards determinist explanations. The emphasis upon the localized socially situated practices of learners and teachers rescues agency from such a danger. The concern with the enhancement of practice leads the writers to propose six principles that should underpin the improvement of learning in FE:

A). Improving learning entails more than increasing its effectiveness. It is important to supplement judgements about learning effectiveness with judgements about the value of learning, and to make issues of effectiveness subordinate to issues of value.

B). There are many different positive learning processes and outcomes, beyond the achievement of a qualification. Different groups and different individuals may appropriately value different things. There is a need to support diversity of such positive learning, as well as recognising that learning can be harmful.

C). Improving the effectiveness of learning entails modifying learning cultures, for example by increasing functional synergies and reducing dysfunctional tensions.

D). In enhancing learning culture, 'what works' is often localised and context specific. Attempts to impose rigid standard procedures are often negative rather than positive in effect.

E). Because of D, improving learning in FE entails creating maximum space for localised initiative, creativity and professional judgement, and creating more synergistic cultures to support and reward such initiatives.

F). The improvement of learning requires a reflectively critical understanding at all levels of intervention: government, college, tutor and, where possible, student. (2005, pp. 9–10)

These broader principles sit alongside other principles of procedures for improving learning in further education that are concerned with: maximizing student agency and tutor professionalism, improving pedagogy and finally with enhancing positive aspects of the learning culture. On one level there is nothing particularly radical about these aspirations as they sit firmly within models of student-centred and progressive practice. Yet on another level the interest in transforming teaching and learning within the sector could rest with a more radical agenda. These authors are aware of the importance of the social structure in the generation of educational inequality. Their intervention could be construed as attempting to subvert and undermine reproductive processes. If learning and teaching is improved in the sector this will offer more stimulating and engaging pedagogic contexts for learners and by doing so may interrupt processes of class reproduction. In a sense Hodkinson alludes to this when discussing bidding for research funds:

> In order to win research funding, we describe our work in ways we do not believe, and which do not fully reflect what we intend to do. We tell cover stories, to bridge between our ecologies of practice and the current sacred stories (Clandinin and Connelly, 1996) of the new orthodoxy. (Hodkinson, 2004, p. 22)

The subtext might be that along the way subversive practices may be developed, herein lying an aspirational politics – a politics of hope. If education is thought of as a site of struggle, one in which inequality is produced, interventions within the classroom may serve to interrupt this process. In this way attempts to transform learning cultures within further education may have a subversive edge. After all it would be risible to evacuate the classroom, or indeed education, as a site of struggle. It would also be deeply problematic to constitute educational struggles as marginal as against those occurring within production or at the site of waged labour, particularly within the current context.

Lingard and colleagues' (Hayes *et al.*, 2005) work in Australian schools similarly sought to intervene in pedagogic relations, and as with the former project aimed to examine good pedagogic practice seeking to develop a model of productive/authentic pedagogy that would offer disadvantaged learners challenging and demanding experiences. Yet Lingard *et al.* (2003a, b) are very careful to qualify their interest in pedagogic relations. Although they strongly argue that teachers make a difference and that they can thereby subvert or at least interrupt reproductive processes, suggesting this far outweighs any other factors deriving from within the school. They go to some lengths recognizing the difficulties facing teachers, specifically noting the performative context in which pedagogic practices are located. Nevertheless they argue forcefully that intellectually challenging and demanding pedagogic relations are pivotal to social justice and crucial for learners drawn from disadvantaged groups. Privileged students can draw upon their family's cultural capital to compensate for school failings, whereas disadvantaged students rarely have such access (Reay *et al.*, 2005).

Whilst their pedagogic model is predicated upon a commitment to social justice, it does encounter a number of problems. One of the difficulties with Lingard *et al.*'s analysis is that whilst there is a sophisticated understanding of pedagogy and the surrounding constraints, it nevertheless veers towards a model which plays down social contestation and antagonism within and to some extent outside education. It is this tendency that results in their approach having much in common with progressive education. A similar point can be made in relation to the work of Hodkinson and others in *TLC*.

There is however a tension in these analyses that allows them to be read in a number of different ways. They can simultaneously point towards radical interventions and an aspirational politics on the one hand, yet comfortably rest with a conservatively oriented modernizing agenda. In this latter case they can veer towards consensual understandings that play down social antagonism and contestation within education.

One form of conservative modernization would argue performativity and its application to the activities of learners and teachers has run its course. That is to say, a focus upon narrow target setting for lecturers is no longer a valid model for continuous improvement. In the same way an argument could be developed that suggests narrow outcome-led learning is out of kilter with the needs of a knowledge economy. This position advocates that pedagogic relations need to be freed up, so that learners are able to develop to their full potential and be in a position to contribute to the wider society and economy. This argument suggests that interventions based upon technical rationality are deeply flawed and in need of modernization. Such arguments could come to rest alongside the rhetoric surrounding competitiveness and lifelong learning. There is an affinity with the apparent need for creativity and the requirement to develop knowledge-workers of the future. There is an inevitable tension between these arguments and those of the authors I have discussed earlier. Without an overt engagement with the politics and forms of contestation characteristic of education and the relation of these to the wider social formation, there is a danger that these arguments for improvement could easily fold into a conservative modernization. A sort of double subversion can arise through which potentially subversive practices become themselves subverted in a conservative direction.

An argument that focuses upon technical rationality serves to set up the counter argument as its opposite. Technical rationality becomes the 'other' to progressive or radical forms, whereas rather than being oppositional there may be a synergy of both with capitalist relations. The following passage drawn from the 2006 white paper on further education could easily rest alongside an argument emphasizing the transformation of teaching and learning in the sector:

> FE has a good record of reaching out to those who are difficult to engage. Nonetheless, if we are to meet the skill demands of future economic growth and employment, then we need to address the cultural, social and economic factors which can limit aspiration and participation. We have to engage not only those learners and employers who already see how skills and qualifications can help them, but the millions who regard education and training as having nothing of value to offer them. (DfES, 2006, p. 34)

Although the white paper is set within an economistic framework derived from the competitiveness settlement and continues to be wedded to performance management, it nevertheless contains moments that presage progressive and transformative educational practices, albeit set within a capitalist hegemony.

Whilst pedagogic relations within further education need to be examined alongside the broader patterns of educational relations of which they are a part, they also need to be placed within the wider socio-economic context. In other words they need to be thought about in relation to the social structure. If we wish to interrupt reproductive processes we need to build connections between institutional sites and the wider socio-economic context in which these processes are located. This becomes particularly important when we wish to address the radicalization of practice.

Towards an expansive practice

Learners are located within a socio-economic structure characterized by iterative processes that serve to reproduce inequality and the privileges of those already advantaged. Following the end of the Second World War there was an expansion in middle-class occupations that provided opportunities of upward mobility for members of the working class. In recent decades the occupational structure has changed such that, 'The rate of inter-generational mobility is now in decline' (Thompson and Lawson, 2006, p. 3).

> Relative social mobility in the UK had fallen over the closing decades of the 20th century. In particular a number of studies examined cohorts of children born in 1958 and 1970, concluding that there was a much stronger association for the latter group between where they started out in life and where they ended up than for those born in 1958, indicating that relative mobility across generations has declined in the last two decades. (Fabian Commission, 2006, p. 14)

This decline in mobility has rested alongside the increasing insecurity that surrounds formerly secure middle-class occupational positions. Ainley (2005a, b) refers to a relatively insecure working/middle class, and Thompson and Lawson suggest that: 'in the hour glass economy, jobs are being created at the top end, but most job growth is at the bottom in low skill, low wage service jobs – the middle is being squeezed' (2006, p. 4). These processes articulate with the continued salience of class origins, albeit mediated by gender and race, on educational performance. This provides the socio-economic context in which young people are placed, as well as shaping the educational institutions in which they study.

It is important to note that examples of good practice must be set within this wider context. There are several reasons why this is important and that serve to illustrate the need for an expansive understanding of practice. These arguments coalesce around the notion of education as a positional good. Educational qualifications and experiences can be conceived as positional goods that, whilst in short supply, confer advantage. The expansion of educational opportunities for those previously excluded has to be thought of in this context. Widening participation for those formerly excluded from education, whilst opening up opportunities also feeds into a credentialism in which higher-level qualifications become a requirement for those occupations where lower-level qualifications were formerly acceptable. The expansion of higher education is a case in point. The former relationship between graduateness and gaining middle-class employment is now neither secure nor sustainable. Increasingly graduates find themselves employed in jobs that were formerly considered not to require a degree. However alongside these processes run others which place emphasis on personal characteristics, that is to say on dispositions deriving from graduates' class, gender and ethnicity, as well as their degree discipline and where they studied.

Pedagogic practices will vary and whilst it will be possible to disseminate what has been learned from research on pedagogy, this will be uneven. Learners who have encountered high-quality pedagogy will be at some advantage. The individualization of educational and economic relations means that this will often be set apart from the wider patterning of educational relations. Such learners may gain some competitive advantage over their peers, and in a sense this process leads to intra-class differentiation. These notions have an affinity with meritocracy and illustrate the need to place educational relations in a wider context. If we fail to place interventions into practice within this wider context they can readily fold over, or become forms of conservative modernization. To offset such a possibility an expansive notion of practice is helpful. It draws together an institutional concern with social justice with the wider socio-economic context through recognition of the political economy of education.

Another way of thinking about these connections is to recognize different sites or levels of struggle, education being but one site that is itself differentiated. There is a need to draw together these educational struggles with others in the wider society. This would allow the development of a counter hegemonic bloc or social movement aiming to transform the social formation towards social justice. Buras and Apple remind us:

> Educational struggles are closely connected to conflicts in larger economic, political, and cultural arenas. Thus, the steadily growing influence of rightist positions in each of these arenas is pronounced and has had major effects in education and the politics of identity and culture, struggles over the production, distribution, and reception of

curriculum, and the connections between national and international mobilizations. Together, these domains form the 'stage' on which the political theatre of education is currently unfolding. (2006, p. 12)

It is also important to conceive of social and economic policy as inextricably connected to educational policy. The separation of education from the former serves to narrow its focus and leads to its depoliticization, a wider understanding offers a corrective to this position. In addition recognition of the relationship between social and economic policy to education illustrates their impact upon educational processes. Anyon (2005) commenting on the USA suggests:

If ... the macro-economy deeply affects the quality of urban education, then perhaps we should re-think what 'counts' as educational policy. Rules and regulations regarding teaching, curriculum, and assessment certainly count; but, perhaps policies that maintain high levels of urban poverty and segregation should be part of the educational policy panoply as well – for these have consequences for urban education at least as profound as curriculum and pedagogy. (2005, p. 3)

And importantly she notes that:

It is important for educators, public policy analysts, and practitioners to take hold of the fact that economic policies yield widespread low-waged work even among an increasingly educated workforce. (p. 29)

This phenomenon is as apparent in the UK as it is in the USA and provides part of the wider context in which young people learn and study (Barry, 2005). It is important that connections are made between educational practice and wider social struggles, and this is why an expansive notion of practice is required. Educational processes cannot be fully understood if they are not set against economic and social practices taking place within the wider society. Educational struggles need to be lodged within a social movement that seeks to undermine oppressive and exploitative relations in order to extend social justice and democracy throughout society.

A starting point would be with the social democratic critique of existing social structures. Barry (2005) in his discussion of the UK and USA illustrates the damaging consequences of a rampant neo-liberalism. Anyon (2005) similarly indicates the negative effects of US economic and social policy upon the poor. In addition a more mainstream analysis would describe the perverse consequences of neo-liberalism, not only for the economy but also for society as a whole. Such a critique would argue that in those societies marked by wide disparities in income and wealth there are lower levels of trust and higher levels of criminality than in those having less inequality (Wilkinson, 2006). Those societies where there are significant inequalities in income and wealth encourage risk adverse behaviour amongst the poorer members of society, for example young people may be unwilling to acquire the debts that will arise while studying in higher education, leading to the loss of talent and creativity (Baker *et al.*, 2004). Even in its own terms high levels of inequality run counter to the interests of a dynamic capitalism, and this is why progressive interventions into education may unintentionally align with a modernizing agenda. A social democratic critique only takes us so far and needs to align with one rooted within radical democracy, forming part of 'non-reformist reforms'. These reforms, when successful, 'change more than the specific institutional features that they target' and 'alter the terrain upon which later struggles will be waged' (Fraser, 2003, p. 79).

Conclusion

This chapter has argued that a critique of the technical rationality of research and substantive work within PCET can take us only so far. This critique sets up progressive and radical work as the 'other' to research located within technical rationality. However the former can as easily sit alongside a modernizing capitalism as the latter. The individualization of educational relations as well as elements of the competitive settlement calling for creativity and the development of a wide range of social and intellective skills align more comfortably with apparently progressive and radical work. The examination of the nature of practice argued that this should be understood expansively and located within the wider pattern of educational and social relations. The consequence of this argument is that radicalized educational practices need to be connected to wider social struggle. If this does not occur the localized and situated nature of educational practice opens it to conservative appropriation, feeding into the differentiation and individualization surrounding educational relations. The formation of a social movement predicated on social justice would support radical practice within and outside education. Such a movement would challenge economic and social relations antithetical to equality and would call for the transformation, not only of learning and teaching within FE but also of economic and social structures of the wider social formation.

Note

1 The Further Education Unit, a state quango, was established to promote, encourage and develop the efficient provision of further education in the UK.

8
Conclusion

Throughout the twentieth century and into the early years of the twenty-first a strong connection has been established between education, economics and social justice. For politicians and policy-makers a successful education system creates the human capital that is the prerequisite for a vibrant and dynamic economy, one that delivers social justice and societal well-being. Each of these themes is problematic, as are the connections made between them, being predicated upon a very particular understanding of economic relations and the manner in which capitalist societies are thought to develop. In each case the associations made are problematic and at best one-sided. This becomes apparent when we examine the manner in which competitiveness has been set alongside the development of human and social capital.

The formation of a workforce able to add value to productive processes is rhetorically construed as the route to competitiveness. In addition such a strategy, if successful (or so it is claimed), would create an employment structure marked by value-added labour. In other words, there would be a shift away from unskilled and semi-skilled labour towards higher levels of skill. This is the terrain on which we encounter the knowledge/information worker. The validity of this is overstated, at best partial and certainly deeply ideological. A positive association between competitiveness, a dynamic capitalism and social justice is rhetorically appealing, having a common-sense ring. But this association is largely fictitious and is undermined by the practices of a neo-liberal capitalism. It is unlikely that the economy, if it were to follow its current trajectory, would be able to undermine patterns of inequality present within society.

It is important to acknowledge that the state is not quite as impotent as supporters of globalization claim. Yet the notion that globalization is an incontestable fact of economic life has an important ideological function as it serves to legitimate a neo-liberal framework within which the English and many Western economies are set. It justifies the dislocations that arise as a result of neo-liberal economics and places the onus upon the individual and their community to respond creatively to processes of change that cannot in any serious way be resisted but that demand appropriate responses. Such ideas are pivotal to the persuasive power of the competitive settlement, contributing to the hegemony of capitalist relations.

The preceding ideas function as persuasive fictions, deflecting criticism from the failings of the economy on to the individual, their community and education system. Some years ago Finn and Frith (1981) discussed the manner in which an economic crisis was transmogrified into an educational one. In the current conjuncture the same processes are at play whereby the demands of the economy are seen as given and it is up to the individual, their community and education system to adapt and respond accordingly. There are two points that need to be made, both of which recognize the ideological thrust of these arguments. First, the way in which the labour process is imagined in these arguments is at best incomplete. The skill mix at the site of waged labour is shaped through struggle as well as by the regional and national context within which it is set. There is no automatic trajectory towards upskilling. Indeed the low-skills route can just as easily deliver profit for employers. Second, the notion of skill is malleable and open to a range of different interpretations. These can shift from the technical through to the dispositional as well as to the aesthetics of labour. The way in which skill is understood especially in arguments that address transferable or personal skills is rather different from those that are more narrowly focused on technical aspects. In addition there is no economic dynamic that offers high-skilled work to the majority of the workforce. Indeed it has been argued that where there has been growth in the labour market it has been in unskilled and semi-skilled labour in the service sector. It is of course possible to describe some of this work in shops, restaurants and bars as skilled, if emphasis is placed upon personal and aesthetic skills. This however serves to illustrate the malleability of the term as well as its ideological uses.

There is a link between the preceding arguments and those that emphasize the situational basis of workplace knowledge. This argument suggests that in a turbulent economic environment, characterized by rapid economic change, the development of work-based knowledge is crucial to the competitiveness of the firm. The basis upon which these arguments are developed is one of a consensus between the interests of employers and employees. These arguments also resonate with those frequently made by employers who claim the education system fails to address their needs appropriately. There are two elements to these arguments that need to be addressed. First, the critique that argues that education, at whatever level, should be aligned more closely to the needs of the economy so that it develops the forms of disposition required by employers. This argument has had a profound impact upon education and is manifest in the concerns with personal or transferable skills, which include the ability to learn. Knowledge within this context becomes far less certain and thus dispositional orientations assume a far greater significance than would formerly have been the case.

Second, the interest in work-based knowledge and the development of appropriate dispositions for waged labour are associated with social justice through the development of vocational pathways for disaffected young people. The intention is to provide vocational pathways that open up progression routes to foundation degrees and beyond. The intention is to use the vocational orientations of young people to reintegrate them into education and in this way open up opportunities from which they would have been excluded. Such a strategy has an apparent concern with social cohesion and inclusion but it is unlikely that this will provide a route to significant upward mobility or indeed a substantial expansion of opportunity for the majority of those concerned. It rests firmly with a concern to habituate young people to the rigours of employment and to prepare them for their position within waged labour.

Work-based learning and work-based knowledge through their situational basis are strongly tied to employer interests for whom their significance lies in the contribution made to the success of the firm concerned. While the experience of work carries a particular pedagogy, debates that focus upon work-based learning are tied to the enhancement of work-related processes. This means that learning and knowledge related to oppression, exploitation and social antagonism surrounding waged labour is sidelined. Indeed organizations that could be construed in these terms are viewed as antithetical to learning. There is a need to debunk work-based experiences and to interrogate them for their progressive and radical possibilities. However, such a project is partly compromised by the way in which knowledge is conceived as situationally specific, truncating levels of generalization.

These ideas have an impact upon the manner in which the curriculum is conceived. If knowledge is arbitrary, uncertain and lacking in any real objectivity, educational processes and the curriculum need to acknowledge this. This type of argument valuably problematizes knowledge and calls for an interrogation of the social interests that it represents. A recognition of this can lead to education processes validating the ability to learn as well as the development of a range of personal and social skills that enable the individual to participate effectively within the society. Paradoxically, whilst these arguments may validate creative and innovative thinking, they nevertheless rest and can easily conjoin with the interest of a modernized capitalism. Against this type of position arguments that operate with a social realist understanding of knowledge can at least recognize that some forms of academic knowledge offer progressive possibilities. This can be developed into a type of really useful knowledge that can be drawn upon in the pursuit of an anti-capitalist project committed to the furtherance of social justice. It is important that the spaces within the curriculum and pedagogic processes which enable the learner to encounter such arguments are held open; otherwise learning can easily become reduced to a form of 'learning to labour', capitalist education. Academic as well as other popular forms of knowledge can be interrogated by learners and teachers for their good sense. Dialogically learners and teachers may seek out the progressive potential of such knowledge so that it can be appropriated in the struggle for social justice. The point is that popular and academic forms of knowledge are Janus-faced and therefore need to be bent to progressive ends. Learner engagement is pivotal to this process with various forms of knowledge being a resource to be used to make sense of wider social relations.

Ironically policy rhetoric, in the current conjuncture, celebrates the need for innovation and creativity. This is embodied in the call for competitiveness and the development of an economy capable of competing in the global market, that demands a labour force able to adapt and respond swiftly to ever changing conditions. The lived experience of those working within PCET is very different from that perceived to be characteristic of the information/knowledge worker required by the new capitalism (Sennett, 2006). The irony is that those working within the sector are to educate the creative, adaptive and innovatory workers required by the new capitalism. However, for many of those teaching within further education their working lives have become characterized by performative practices. Surveillance and policing are consistent features of such work and result in demoralization and a tendency to undermine the professionalism and commitment of those working in the sector.

It would be quite wrong to see the past as some sort of golden age to which we should return (Simmons, 2006). Given the conditions in which education is placed this is unlikely and, more importantly, would not offer a progressive politics.

Rather, we should consider the terrain on which teachers labour within PCET and interrogate these conditions for their possibilities. Whilst teacher's labour may have become more closely policed, there will still be spaces that could be appropriated for progressive and critical practice. The very rhetoric that celebrates innovation and creativity is one that can be appropriated and used to justify the development of radical practice. The language of deprofessionalization, proletarianization and reprofessionalization is too crude to fully capture teachers' lived experience. We need to recognize the way in which these processes are unevenly lived, seeking out the progressive and attempting to minimize the regressive.

Currently the language of targets, performativity and close-in surveillance is seen as counter productive, at least by some elements within the state. There is a move towards 'light touch' inspections and the willingness to offer more autonomy to successful institutions and teachers. This is frequently portrayed as a reinstigation of relations of trust and a return to a form of professionalism and collegiality. It is however a conditional trust given on the basis of continued successful performance. There are two points to be made. First, these practices are set on a very particular terrain that coheres with modernizing interests. Second, the space offered may function more effectively as a form of control and surveillance through its impact on the subjectivities of those involved by shaping understandings of good or acceptable practice. Or put more correctly, the way this is defined through processes of institutional audit that constitute a regime of truth.

The development of a teaching identity organized around the notion of the learning professional is seen as a means of developing a cohesive community amongst lecturers. This, or so it is claimed, provides a basis for solidarity amongst the workforce and serves to overcome existing divisions and fractures. The teaching body within further education is diverse, with lecturers drawing upon a range of vocational and disciplinary cultures that themselves are mediated through classed, gendered and raced processes. The development of the notion of the learning professional offers a means of overcoming these differences. This form of professionalism could become lodged within a wider deliberative community that extends beyond institutional boundaries. For such practices to be effective there is a need to recognize the social antagonisms present within further education and wider society. Without such recognition these practices could easily fold back, becoming a form of conservative modernization. Because of these difficulties it is important to recognize that teaching is a form of work, of waged labour, and that it carries with it a range of contradictions and social antagonisms.

Much of the 1980s and 1990s ethnography that addressed the experiences of learners within the sector drew upon Marxist and socialist feminist reproduction theory. There was a concern to document the manner in which young people were prepared for domestic and waged labour and with the way in which they developed forms of subjectivity that were in alignment with such work. These processes were themselves closely articulated to those of race, class and gender, as well as with forms of masculinity and femininity. This form of analysis has been eclipsed in recent years, whilst at the same time state policy has become more aggressively oriented towards meeting the putative needs of employers, with education, at whatever level, being directed to address this particular goal.

Current explorations of learner experience offer complex analyses that recognize the uncertain conditions facing young people in the economic and social conditions of reflexive or late modernity. This work explores learning cultures and the manner in which young people's identities become transformed through such processes. It overcomes determinist tendencies within theories of reproduction as well as the marginalization of pedagogy and practice. This work provides more nuanced accounts that acknowledge young people's agency and is its greatest strength. Its limitation is that it can easily underplay the significance of structural relations and ignore the social antagonisms present within further education and wider society. A fully politicized account of further education demands the antagonistic relations present within education and the social formation are acknowledged. Such a recognition enables analysis to consider the way in which learner dispositions and identity articulate with the ongoing (re)production of labour power. This would conjoin with an analysis concerned with the way in which class and other differences are continuously produced and 'gets done' through educative processes.

The interest in practice and the improvement of teaching and learning in the sector can align with a concern with social justice. It could be construed as part of an ongoing struggle to undermine reproductive processes and in this way addresses questions of social justice. However, such an interest cannot be restricted to the classroom, or indeed to any particular college or educational institution. One of the ways in which this question can be addressed is by considering different levels of struggle and their articulation to educational relations in particular and inequality in general. Such a standpoint aligns with an expansive notion of practice and argues that this cannot be fully understood without an engagement with the relational context of educational practice. An interest in deliberative processes goes some way to addressing these concerns as it locates practice within a wider political context. The danger is that this can easily fold over to become a form of stakeholder analysis that plays down antagonistic relations and the very real conflicts and struggles surrounding education.

Dialogue and deliberation can point towards the development of a counter hegemonic bloc. It is nevertheless necessary to be attentive to contradictions and the manner in which apparently progressive language can be rearticulated to serve conservative ends. This danger highlights the importance of dialogue, the recognition of social antagonism as well as the need to develop a loosely connected social movement committed to the furtherance of social justice in education and society. Gillborn, whilst discussing racism, writes:

> There is a real danger that we are being seduced (by funding priorities and demands to be 'relevant') into a school-level focus that loses sight of the bigger picture (Thrupp and Wilmott, 2004, after Ozga, 1990). If we *only* focus on the scale of inequity, and school level approaches to addressing it, we lose sight of the most powerful forces operating

at the societal level to sustain and extend these inequalities. (2006, p. 18)

A similar analysis could be more generally applied to PCET and its relationship to inequality. Such an analysis adopting an expansive notion of practice could rest with the pursuit of non-reformist reforms and be able to operate on a number of levels including the classroom, the institution, regional and national contexts and so on. Such a standpoint acknowledges that educational processes cannot be anything other than political and adopts an aspirational politics – a politics of hope.

Well-being and the new capitalism

At the time of writing, whilst the competitive settlement is firmly in place and managerialist forms well established, the negative consequences of neo-liberal economics are becoming increasingly apparent. Although the state remains wedded to performativity, the language of targets, performance indicators and so on, there are embryonic attempts to soften these and ameliorate the crasser effects of neo-liberal economic practices. A number of these softening elements have been long-standing features of New Labour policy, particularly in relation to measures that aim to develop social inclusion and cohesion. In the argument being developed here the efficacy of these policies is not the question being addressed. Rather, these concerns, as with questions of social justice, offer resources that can be marshalled in political struggle and articulated in the formation of counter hegemonic blocs and oppositional social movements.

Sennett argues that the 'new capitalism', albeit found within a minority of organizations, carries three deficits: 'low institutional loyalty, diminishment of informal trust, and weakening of institutional knowledge' (2006, p. 63). There is an affinity between this description and post-Fordism and the call for ever adaptable and responsive workers. Low institutional loyalty is almost a parody of the need for tough choices to ensure the ongoing competitiveness of the firm and economy. Such an argument would serve to justify the closure of plants that are apparently unviable. Sennett also draws attention to the emphasis placed upon 'potential' within the new capitalism, which sits alongside the need for constant innovation and change. These changes carry challenges to work-based identities that are viewed as constantly in transition, not fixed and which fail to provide a strong mooring for individual identity and sense of worth. Thus work-based identities become infinitely malleable and perishable.

The changes deriving from the new capitalism sit alongside those of globalization, for example deindustrialization, the fragmentation of community and the loss of a sense of belonging, etc. The state's response has been to seek to reinstate forms of social solidarity. The notion of social capital is particularly appealing as it provides a strategy to develop networks that can be used to reinvigorate relations of trust, thereby generating higher levels of social solidarity. These moves, as with others, can be appropriated and bent to progressive ends. This is also the case with the renewed interest in older social democratic concerns (see *Renewal*, 2006), as well as the current cross-party interest in the development of societal well-being (Cameron, 2006; Donovan and Halpern, 2002; McAllister, 2005; Shah and Marks, 2004). All of these themes hold progressive possibilities, as can be said for the ongoing concern with environmental and ecological issues that Giddens (1998) has associated with a renewed and up-dated social democracy. All these elements provide ideological resources that can be appropriated in the struggle to transform social and economic relations in the furtherance of social justice.

The current interest in well-being can be seen as a response to the social costs generated by neo-liberalism and has an affinity with concerns about social cohesion and inclusion. This current focus upon well-being has at its centre ways of according value to the individual and communities. That is to say values which validate those transcending the narrowly economic and move beyond the insecurities surrounding waged labour. This emerging project anticipates the development of post-materialist cultures and sustainable economic development. Whilst these concerns hold progressive possibilities the danger is that they are easily co-opted to serve hegemonic interests. Communities and individuals that adjust their expectations in line with the development of post-materialist cultures and sustainable economic development may be reinventing themselves to accept their place within societal relations. This may serve state interests in the development of forms of social solidarity and may legitimate inequitable social structures based upon exploitation and oppression, masking underlying social antagonisms. The Gramscian concepts of 'transformism' and 'passive revolution' are helpful in making sense of these dangers. Johnson and Steinberg comment,

> Transformism does not, however, develop or 'educate' these currents, does not 'bring out the best of them', as it were. It does not base itself within them. Rather it seeks to contain and control popular forces from outside. This may involve making real concessions, but always within the limits of existing social arrangements. At this more 'structural' level, involving socio-economic relations and whole ways of life, passive revolution is an attempt to solve structural problems within the terms of existing structures. An example today might be trying to solve environmental problems without curtailing the production of commodities or contesting the power of big corporations. (2004, p. 13)

Transformist tendencies are present in the way in which the spread of a sense of well-being throughout society is thought to bring with it economic dividends.

> Well-being literature provides many insights into what makes good work. It is in the self-interest of business to promote good work as there are linkages between quality work, productivity, and work retention. (Shah and Marks, 2004, p. 9)

There is a danger that such findings will be separated from the broader arguments of which they are a constitutive part, being rearticulated to serve hegemonic interests. This can be seen in the appropriation of arguments concerned with well-being by Conservative politicians (Cameron, 2006). A similar point could be made about arguments addressing social capital and the development of networks and relations based on trust. These sorts of relations are often seen as both contributing towards a sense of well-being and as leading to a reduction in transaction costs, thereby contributing towards economic efficiency (Donovan and Halpern, 2002; Kay, 1996).

There is a need to work with the progressive possibilities that exist within the current conjuncture. This would entail working with the 'good sense' embodied in social democracy and other social movements and forms. The idea of radical democracy is particularly helpful in that it suggests an aspirational politics which focuses upon the present, constantly seeking to move the social formation in directions of greater social justice and wider democratization. This is a politics of hope (Halpin, 2003). An education system that is wedded to economic imperatives rooted in a capitalist hegemony is unlikely to contribute to such a project. Despite the demands placed on education it is not possible for conservative forces to close down the spaces that exist for struggle. The trick is to address student need, whether in terms of examination success or the development of work-based skills, whilst simultaneously lodging these within an expansive educative project. Such a project seeks to understand and interrogate the social context within which education is placed, recognize the salience of social antagonism whilst at the same time it is committed to the pursuit of social justice.

References

Abel-Smith, B. and Townsend, P. (1965) *The Poor and the Poorest*, London, Bell.

Ainley, P. (2005a) 'For free universities', an Inaugural lecture delivered at the University of Greenwich, 19 January.

— (2005b) Paper presented to Discourse, Power, Resistance Conference, University of Plymouth, Plymouth, 21–23 March.

Ainley, P. and Bailey, B. (1997) *The Business of Learning*, London, Cassell.

Alexiadou, N. (2001) 'Management identities in transition: a case study from further education', *The Sociological Review*, vol. 49, no. 3, 412–35.

Allen, M. (2005a) 'White Paper: tables turned on Tomlinson', *Radical Education Journal*, issue 2, 1.

— (2005b) 'The 14–19 White Paper: a new tripartism', *Post–16 Educator*, issue 26, 3–4.

Althusser, L. (1969) *For Marx*, Harmondsworth, Penguin.

— (1972) 'Ideology and ideological state apparatuses', in Cosin, B. R. (ed.), *Education: Structure and Society*, Harmondsworth, Penguin.

Analysis, (1998) *Doing it Their Way*, transcript of a recorded documentary on Radio 4, 29 June, London, BBC White City, tape number TLN824/98VT1026.

Anyon, J. (2005) *Radical Possibilities: Public Policy, Urban Education and a New Social Movement*, New York, Routledge.

Apple, M. (1979) *Ideology and the Curriculum*, London, Routledge & Kegan Paul.

— (1996) *Cultural Politics and Education*, Buckingham, Open University Press.

— (2001) *Educating the Right Way*, London, RoutledgeFalmer.

— (2004) 'Doing things the "right" way', in Satterthwaite, J., Atkinson, E. and Martin, W. (eds), *Educational Counter-cultures: Confrontations, Images, Visions*, Stoke on Trent, Trentham.

Apple, M. and Buras, K. L. (2006) 'Introduction', in Buras, K. L. and

Apple, M. (eds), *The Subaltern Speak: Curriculum, Power and Educational Struggle*, London, Routledge.

Aronowitz, S. (2006) 'Subaltern in paradise: knowledge production in the corporate academy', Apple, M. and Buras, K. L. (eds), *The Subaltern Speak: Curriculum, Power and Educational Struggles*, London, Routledge.

Aronowitz, S. and Giroux, H. (1986) *Education under Siege*, London, Routledge & Kegan Paul.

Attwood, G., Croll, P. and Hamilton, J. (2003) 'Re-engaging with education', *Research Papers in Education*, vol. 18, no. 1, 75–95.

— (2004) 'Challenging students in further education: themes arising from a study of innovative FE provision for excluded and disaffected young people', *Journal of Further and Higher Education*, vol. 28, no. 1, 107–19.

Audit Commission (1993) *Unfinished Business: Full-time Educational Courses for 16–19-year-olds*, London, HMSO.

Avis, J. (1983) 'ABC and the new vocational consensus, *Journal of Further and Higher Education*, Spring, 23–33.

— (1984) 'Strategies of survival: pre-vocational students in FE', *British Journal of Sociology of Education*, vol. 5, no. 2, 129–51.

— (1985) 'The ambiguities of conformism: academic students in FE', *Sociological Review*, vol. 33, no. 4, 708–40.

— (1991a) 'The strange fate of progressive education', Education Group II, Department of Cultural Studies, University of Birmingham, *Education Limited: Schooling and Training and the New Right since 1979*, London, Unwin Hyman.

— (1991b) 'Curriculum categories and student identities in FE', Education Group II *Education Limited: Schooling and Training and the New Right Since 1979*, London, Unwin Hyman.

— (1993) 'A new orthodoxy, old problems: post–16 reforms', *British Journal of Sociology of Education*, vol. 14, no. 3, 245–60.

— (1996a) 'The myth of the post-Fordist society' in Avis, J., Bloomer, M., Esland, G., Gleeson, D. and Hodkinson, P., *Knowledge and Nationhood: Education, Politics and Work*, London, Cassell.

— (1996b) 'The enemy within: quality and managerialism in education', in Avis, J., Bloomer, M., Esland, G., Gleeson, D. and Hodkinson, P., *Knowledge and Nationhood: Education, Politics and Work*, London, Cassell.

— (1996c) 'Learner identity, vocationalism and global relations: students in FE', *British Journal of Education and Work*, vol. 9, no. 3, 35–46.

— (1997) 'What's this got to do with what I do!' Contradictory views: students in FE', *Journal of Vocational Education and Training*, vol. 49, no. 1, 81–106.

— (1998) '(Im)possible dream: post-Fordism, stakeholding and post-compulsory education', *Journal of Education Policy*, vol. 13, no. 2, 251–63.

— (1999) 'Shifting Identity – New conditions and the transformation of practice: Teaching within post-compulsory education', *Journal of Vocational Education and Training*, vol. 51, no. 2, p. 245–64.

— (2000) 'The forces of Conservatism: New Labour, the third way, reflexive modernisation and social justice', *Education and Social Justice*, vol. 2, no. 3, p. 31–8.

— (2001) 'Educational Research, the Teacher Researcher and Social Justice', *Education and Social Justice*, vol. 3, no. 3, p. 34–42.

— (2002) 'Imaginary friends: managerialism, globalisation and post-compulsory education and training in England', *Discourse: Studies in the Cultural Politics of Education*, vol. 23, no. 1, 75–90.

— (2003) 'Social capital, collective intelligence and expansive learning, thinking through the connections: education and the economy', *British Journal of Education Studies*, vol. 50, no. 3, 308–26.

— (2005) 'Activity theory: transformation and a politics of hope', unpublished paper.

Avis J. and Bathmaker, A.-M. (2006) 'From trainee to FE lecturer: trials and tribulations', *Journal of Vocational Education and Training*, vol. 58, no. 2, 171–89.

Avis, J., Bathmaker, A.-M. and Parsons, J. (2002) 'Communities of practice and the construction of learners in post-compulsory education and training', *Journal of Vocational Education and Training*, vol. 54, no. 1, 27–50.

Avis, J., Bloomer, M., Esland, G., Gleeson, D. and Hodkinson, P. (1996) *Knowledge and Nationhood*, London, Cassell.

Baker, J., Lynch, K., Cantillon, S. and Walsh, J. (2004) *Equality From Theory to Action*, Houndsmill, Palgrave Macmillan.

Ball, C. (1991) *Learning Pays*, London, Royal Society of Arts.

Ball, S. (1993) 'Education markets, choice and social class: the market as a class strategy in the UK and the USA', *British Journal of Sociology of Education*, vol. 14, no. 1, 3–20.

Ball, S. J. (2003) *Class Strategies and the Education Market: The Middle Class and Social Advantage*, London, RoutledgeFalmer.

— (2004) 'The necessity and violence of theory, paper presented to the *British Educational Research Association Annual Conference*, UMIST, Manchester, September.

Ball, S. J., Maguire, M. and Macrae, S. (2000) *Choice, Pathways and Transitions Post–16*, London, RoutledgeFalmer.

Barnett, R. (2000) 'Working Knowledge', Garrick, J. and Rhodes, C. (eds) *Research and Knowledge at Work*, London, Routledge.

Barry, B. (2005) *Why Social Justice Matters*, Cambridge, Polity.

Bates, I. (1990) '"No bleeding whining minnies": the role of YTS in gender and class reproduction', *British Journal of Education and Work*, vol. 3, no. 2, 91–110.

— (1991) 'Closely observed training: an exploration of links between social structures, training and identity', *International Studies in Sociology of Education*, vol. 1, no. 2, 225–43.

Bates, I., Clarke, J., Cohen, P., Finn, D., Moore, R. and Willis, P. (eds) (1984) *Schooling for the Dole? The New Vocationalism*, London, Macmillan.

Bates, I. and Riseborough, G. (eds) (1993) *Youth and Inequality*, Milton Keynes, Open University Press.

Bathmaker, A.-M. (2001) 'GNVQ: "It's the perfect education". GNVQ, lifelong learning and the experience of foundation students', *Journal of Vocational Education and Training*, vol. 53, no. 1, 81–100.

Bathmaker, A.-M. and Avis, J. (forthcoming) '"How do I cope with that?" The challenge of "schooling" cultures in further education for trainee FE lecturers', *British Educational Research Journal*.

Batten, L. and Skinner, M. (1997) *The Lecturer's Job: A Survey of Conditions of Service in New Universities and Higher Education*, Commissioned by Natfhe, Epsom, Crossbow Research.

Beane, J. A. and Apple, M. (1999) *Democratic Schools: Lessons from the Chalk Face*, Buckingham, Open University Press.

Beck, J. and Young, M. (2005) 'The assault on the professions and the restructuring of academic and professional identities: a Bernsteinian analysis', *British Journal of Sociology of Education*, vol. 26, no. 2, 183–97.

Beck, U. (1992) *The Risk Society*, Cambridge, Polity.

— (1999) *World Risk Society*, Cambridge, Polity.

Beckett, D. (2000) 'Eros and the virtual: enframing working knowledge through technology', Symes, C. and McIntyre, J. (eds), *Working Knowledge: The New Vocationalism and Higher Education*, Buckingham, Open University Press.

Beckett, F. (2005) 'Blair's way', *Management Today*, 24 February, www.clickmt/public/news/, accessed 23 June.

Bentley, T. and Wilsdon, J. (2003) 'Introduction: the adaptive state', in Bentley and Wilsdon (eds), *The Adaptive State: Strategies for Personalising the Public Realm*, London, Demos.

Bernstein, B. (1977) *Class, Codes and Control, Vol, 3*, London, Routledge & Kegan Paul.

Biesta, G. (2004) 'Against learning: reclaiming a language for education in an age of learning', *Nordisk Padagogik*, vol. 24, no. 1, 70–82.

Blair, T. (2004a) 'Building the opportunity society', speech at Beveridge Hall, University of London, 11 October.

— (2004b) 'My passion to transform education is undimmed', Fabian lecture, Institute of Education, London, 7 July, www.fabian-society.org.uk/press_office/.

Bloomer, M. (1997) *Curriculum Making in Post–16 Education: The Social Conditions of Studentship*, London, Routledge.

— (2001) 'Young lives, learning and transformation: some theoretical considerations', *Oxford Review of Education*, vol. 27, no. 3, 429–49.

Bloomer, M. and Hodkinson, P. (1999) *College Life: The Voice of the Learner*, FEDA Report, London, FEDA.

— (2001) 'Learning careers and cultural capital: adding a social and longitudinal dimension into our understanding of learning, in Nata, R. (ed.), *Progress in Education, vol. 5*, New York, Nova Science Publishers.

Bloomer, M. and James, D. (2001) 'Research for educational practice: the promise of the transforming learning cultures in further education project', paper presented at the *Fifth Annual Conference of the Learning and Skills Research Network, Robinson College*, Cambridge, 5–7 December.

Boud, D. and Symes, C. (2000) 'Learning for real: work-based education in universities', in Symes, C. and McIntrye, J. (eds), *Working Knowledge: The New Vocationalism and Higher Education*, Buckingham, Open University Press.

Boudon, R. (1974) *Education, Opportunity and Social Inequality*, London, Wiley.

Bourdieu, P. (1998) *Contre-feux*, Paris, Liber Raison d'Agir.

— (2002) *Distinction: A Social Critique of the Judgement of Taste*, London, Routledge.

Bourdieu, P. and Passeron, J.-C. (1977) *Reproduction in Education, Society and Culture*, London, Sage.

Bourdieu, P. and Wacquant, L. (1992) *An Invitation to Reflexive Sociology*, Cambridge, Polity.

Bowe, R., Ball, S. J. with Gold, A. (1992) *Reforming Education and Changing Schools: Case Studies in Policy Sociology*, London, Routledge.

Bowles, G. and Gintis, H. (1976) *Schooling in Capitalist America*, London, Routledge & Kegan Paul.

Braverman, H. (1974) *Labor and Monopoly Capital: The Degradation of Work in the Twentieth Century*, New York, Monthly Review Press.

Brown, G. (2000) 'My vision of a fairer Britain for everyone', *The Times* 3 June, 22.

Brown, J. S., Collins, A. and Duguid, P. (1989) 'Situated cognition and the culture of learning', *Educational Researcher*, vol. 18, no. 1, 32–42.

Brown, P. (1987) *Schooling Ordinary Kids: Inequality, Unemployment, and the New Vocationalism*, London, Tavistock.

— (2001) 'Globalization and the political economy of high skills', in Brown, P., Green, A. and Lauder, H. (eds) (2001) *High Skills: Globalization, Competitiveness and Skill Formation*, Oxford, Oxford University Press.

Brown, P., Green, A. and Lauder, H. (eds) (2001) *High Skills: Globalization, Competitiveness and Skill Formation*, Oxford, Oxford University Press.

Brown, P. and Lauder, H. (eds) (1992) *Education for Economic Survival: From Fordism to Post-Fordism*, London, Routledge.

— (2000) 'Human capital, social capital, and collective intelligence, in Baron, S., Field, J. and Schuller, T. (eds), *Social Capital, Critical Perspectives*, Oxford, Oxford University Press.

Callinicos, A. (1999) 'Social theory put to the test of politics: Pierre Bourdieu and Anthony Giddens', *New Left Review*, no. 236, 77–102

Cameron, D. (2006) 'Improving society's sense of well-being is challenge of our times', speech at Google Zeitgeist Europe, Hertfordshire, 22 May.

Castells, M. (2000) *The Rise of the Network Society*, 2nd edn, Oxford, Blackwells.

Cathcart, M. and Esland, G. (1985) 'The compliant-creative worker: the ideological reconstruction of the school leaver', in Barton, L. and Walker, S. (eds), *Education and Social Change*, London, Croom Helm.

Centre for Educational Research and Innovation (2002) *Educational Research and Development in England: Background Report*, JT00132176, Paris, OECD.

Channel 4, (2003) *7.00 Channel 4 News*, 17 October.

Chapman, J. (2002) *System Failure*, London, Demos.

Chappell, C., Farrel, L., Scheeres, H. and Solomon, N. (2000) 'The organisation of identity: four cases', in Symes, C. and McIntyre, J. (eds), *Working Knowledge: The New Vocationalism and Higher Education*, Buckingham, Open University Press.

Clandinin, J. and Connelly, M. (eds) (1996) *Teachers' Professional Knowledge Landscapes*, New York, Teachers College Press.

Clarke, J., Cochrane, A. and McLaughlin (eds) (1994) *Managing Social Policy*, London, Sage.

Clarke, J. and Newman, J. (1997) *The Managerial State*, London, Sage.

Coates, K. and Silburn, R. (1970) *Poverty: The Forgotten Englishmen*, Harmondsworth, Penguin.

Codd, J. (1999) 'Educational reform, accountability and the culture of distrust', *New Zealand Journal of Educational Studies*, vol. 34, no. 1, 45–53.

Cole, P. (2000) 'Men, women and changing managements of further education', *Journal of Further and Higher Education*, vol. 24, no. 2, 203–15.

Coleman, S. and Keep, E. (2001) *Background Literature Review of PIU Project on Workforce Development*, London, Cabinet Office, Strategy Unit.

Colley, H. (2006) 'Learning to labour with feeling: class, gender and emotion in childcare education and training', *Contemporary Issues in Early Childhood*, vol. 7, no. 1, 15–29.

Colley, H. and Hodkinson, P. (2001) 'Problems with *Bridging the Gap*: the reversal of structure and agency in addressing social exclusion', *Critical Social Policy*, vol. 21, no. 3, 335–59.

Colley, H., James, D., Tedder, M. and Diment, K. (2003) 'Learning as becoming in vocational education and training: class, gender and the role of vocational habitus', *Journal of Vocational Education and Training*, vol. 55, no. 4, 471–98.

Colley, H., Wahlberg, M. and Gleeson, D. (2005) 'Improving teaching and learning in further education: towards a genealogy', paper presented to the *British Educational Research Association Annual Conference*, Glamorgan, 15–17 September.

Connell, R. W. (1983) *Which Way Is Up? Essays on Sex, Class and Culture*, Sydney, Allen & Unwin.

Cousins, S. (2002) *Improving Colleges through Action Research*, London, LSDA.

Crowther, J., Galloway, V. and Martin, I. (eds) (2005) *Popular Education: Engaging the Academy*, Leicester, niace.

Dale, R., Bowe, R., Harris, D., Loveys, M., Moore, R., Shilling, C., Sikes, P., Trevitt, J. and Valsecchi, V. (1990) *The TVEI Story: Policy, Practice and Preparation for the Workforce*, Milton Keynes, Open University Press.

Davies, P. (2000) 'The relevance of systematic reviews to educational policy and practice', *Oxford Review of Education*, vol. 26, nos 3 and 4, 365–78.

Dearing, R. (1996) *Review of Qualifications for 16–19 year olds*, London, SCAA.

Deem, R., Ozga, J. and Prichard, C. (2000) 'Managing further education: is it still men's work too?' *Journal of Further and Higher Education*, vol. 24, no. 2, 231–50.

Derber, C. (1983) 'Managing professionals: ideological proletarianisation and post industrial labour', *Theory and Society*, vol. 12, no. 2, 309–41.

DfEE, (1997) *Excellence in Schools*, Cm 3681, London, HMSO.

— (1998a) *The Learning Age: A Renaissance for a New Britain. A Summary* http//www.lifelonglearning.co.uk.

— (1998b) *The Learning Age: A Renaissance for a New Britain*, Cm 3790, London, The Stationery Office.

— (1998c) *Further Education for the New Millennium: Responses to the Kennedy Report*, London, DfEE.

— (2001b) *Raising Standards: teaching in Further Education*, Nottingham, DfEE.

DfES (2001a) *Schools Achieving Success*, London, DfES.

— (2002a) *Success for All: Reforming Further Education and Training, Our Vision of the Future*, London, DfES.

— (2002b) *14–19: Extending Opportunities, Raising Standards*, Cm 5342, London, HMSO.

— (2003) *14–19: Opportunity and Excellence*, Nottingham, DfES Publications.

— (2004) *Five-year Strategy for Children and Learners*, Cm 6272, London, DfES.

— (2005a) *14–19 Education and Skills*, Cm 6476, London, DfES.

— (2005b) *Skills: Getting on in Business, Getting on at Work*, Cm 6483-1, London, DfES.

— (2006) *Further Education: Raising Skills, Improving Life Chances*, Cm 6768, Norwich, HMSO.

Dolby, N. and Dimitriadis, G. (2004) 'Learning to labor in new times: an introduction' in Dolby, N., Dimitriadis, G. and Willis, P. (eds) (2004) *Learning to Labor in New Times*, London, RoutledgeFalmer.

Donovan, N. and Halpern, D. (2002) *Life Satisfaction: The State of Knowledge and Implications for Government*, London, Cabinet Office Strategy Unit.

Douglas, J. W. B. (1967) *The Home and the School*, London, Panther.

Earley, P. (1994) *Lecturers' Workload and Factors affecting Stress levels: A Research Report from the NFER*, Slough, Natfhe.

Ecclestone, K. (1999) 'Care or control? Defining learners' needs for lifelong learning', *British Journal of Education Studies*, vol. 47, no. 4, 332–377.

— (2002) *Learning Autonomy in Post–16 Education: The Politics and Practice of Formative Assessment*, London, RoutledgeFalmer.

Education Group (1981) *Unpopular Education: Schooling and Social Democracy in England since 1944*, London, Hutchinson.

Education Group II (1991) *Education Limited: Schooling and Training and the New Right since 1979*, London, Unwin Hyman.

Edwards, R. (1993) *Mature Women Students*, London, Taylor & Francis.

Edwards, R. and Usher, R. (2000) 'Research on work, research at work: postmodern perspectives', in Garrick, J. and Rhodes, C. (eds), *Research and Knowledge at Work*, London, Routledge.

Edwards, T., Fitz-Gibbon, C., Hardman, F., Haywood, R. and Meagher, N. (1997) *Separate but Equal? A Levels and GNVQs*, London, Routledge.

Elliott, G. (1996a) *Crisis and Change in Vocational Education and Training*, London, Jessica Kingsley.

— (1996b) 'Why is research invisible in further education?', *British Education Research Journal*, vol. 22, no. 1 101–11.

Elliott, J. (2001a) 'Characteristics of performative cultures: their central paradoxes and limitations as resources for educational reform', in Gleeson, D. and Husbands, C. (eds), *The Performing School: Managing, Teaching and Learning in a Performance Culture*, London, RoutledgeFalmer.

— (2001b) 'Making evidence-based practice educational', *British Educational Research Journal*, vol. 27, no. 5, 555–74.

Engeström, Y. (2001) 'Expansive learning at work: toward an activity theoretical reconceptualisation', *Journal of Education and Work*, vol. 14, no. 1, 133–56.

EPPI (2001) *Review Group Manual*, London, EPPI-centre.

Evans, J. and Benefield, P. (2001) 'Systematic reviews of educational research: does the medical model fit?', *British Educational Research Journal*, vol. 27, no. 5, 527–41.

Fabian Commission (2006) *Narrowing the Gap: The Fabian Commission on Life Chances and Child Poverty*, London, Fabian Society.

FEFC (1997a) 'Validating self-assessment', *Circular 97/12*.

— (1997b) 'Self-assessment and inspections', *Circular 97/13*.

FE Now! (1997) 'My kind of town', issue 36, April, 9.

FENTO (1999) *Standards for teaching and supporting learning in further education in England and Wales*, London, FENTO.

FEU (1979) *A Basis for Choice*, London, FEU.

— (1992) *A Basis for Credit?*, London, FEU.

Fielding, M. (1988) 'Democracy and fraternity: towards a new paradigm of the comprehensive school', in Lauder, H. and Brown, P. (eds), *Education: In Search of a Future*, London, Falmer.

Finegold, D., Keep, E., Miliband, D., Raffe, D., Spours, K. and Young, M. (1990) *A British Baccalaureate: Overcoming Divisions between Education and Training*, London, IPPR.

Finegold, D. and Soskice, D. (1988) 'The failure of training in Britain: analysis and prescription', *Oxford Review of Economic Policy*, vol. 4, no. 3, 21–53.

Finn, D. (1987) *Training without Jobs*, London, Macmillan.

Finn, D. and Frith, S. (1981) 'Unit 4 Education and the labour market', Block 1 *The State and the Politics of Education*, Part 2, Milton Keynes, Open University Press.

Foster, A. (2005) *Realising the Potential: A Review of the Role of Further Education Colleges*, Annesley, DfES, Crown.

Foucault, M. (1980) 'Truth and power', in Gordon, C. (ed.) *Power/knowledge: Selected Interviews and Other Writings 1972–1977*, New York, Pantheon.

Fraser, N. (2003) 'Social justice in the age of identity politics: redistribution, recognition, and participation', in Fraser, N. and Honneth, A. *Redistribution or Recognition? A Political-philosophical Exchange*, London, Verso.

Freire, P. (1972) *Pedagogy of the Oppressed*, Harmondsworth, Penguin.

— (1985) *The Politics of Education: Culture, Power and Liberation*, London, Macmillan.

Fryer, R. H. (1999) *Creating Learning Cultures: Next Steps in achieving the Learning Age*, Second Report of the National Advisory Group for Continuing Education and Lifelong Learning, www.lifelonglearning.co.uk/nagcell2/index.htm.

Fuller, A., Hodkinson, H., Hodkinson, P. and Unwin, L. (2005) 'Learning as peripheral participation in communities of practice: a reassessment of key concepts in workplace learning, *British Educational Research Journal*, vol. 31, no. 1, 49–68.

Fuller, A. and Unwin, L. (2003) 'Learning as apprentices in the contemporary UK workplace: creating and managing expansive and restrictive participation', *Journal of Education and Work*, vol. 16, no. 4, 407–26.

Garrahan, P. and Stewart, P. (1992) *The Nissan Enigma*, London, Mansell.

Garrick, J. (1998) *Informal Learning in the Workplace: Unmasking Human Resource Development*, London, Routledge.

Garrick, J. and Clegg, S. (2000) 'Organizational Gothic: transfusing vitality and transforming the corporate body through work-based learning, in Garrick, J. and Rhodes, C. (eds), *Research and Knowledge at Work*, London, Routledge.

Garrick, J. and Rhodes, C. (eds) (2000) *Research and Knowledge at Work: Perspectives, Case Studies and Innovative Strategies*, London, Routledge.

Geras, N. (1977) 'Althusser's Marxism: an assessment', in *New Left Review* (eds), *Western Marxism: A Critical Reader*, London, in *New Left Review*.

Gewirtz, S. (2002) *The Managerial School: Post-welfarism and Social Justice in Education*, London, Routledge.

— (2004) 'Taking a stand: education policy, sociology and social values', inaugural lecture, King's College London, 5 February.

Gewirtz, S. and Cribb, A. (2003) 'Recent readings of social reproduction', *International Studies in Sociology of Education*, vol. 13, no. 3, 243–59.

Gewirtz, S., Dickson, M., Power, S., Halpin, D. and Whitty, G. (2005) 'The deployment of social capital theory in educational policy and provision: the case of education action zones in England', *British Educational Research Journal*, vol. 31, no. 6, 651–73.

Gibson, R. (1986) *Critical Theory and Education*, London, Hodder & Stoughton.

Giddens, A. (1991) *Modernity and Self-identity*, Cambridge, Polity.

— (1994) *Beyond Left and Right: The Future of Radical Politics*, Cambridge, Polity.

— (1998) *The Third Way: The Renewal of Social Democracy*, Cambridge, Polity.

— (2000) *The Third Way and its Critics*, Cambridge, Polity.

— (2002) *Where Now for New Labour?* Cambridge, Polity.

— (2003) 'Introduction', in Giddens, A. (ed.) *The Progressive Manifesto*, Cambridge, Polity.

Gillborn, D. (2005) 'Education policy as an act of white supremacy: whiteness, critical race theory and education reform', *Journal of Education Policy*, vol. 20, no. 4, 485–505.

— (2006) 'Critical race theory and education: racism and anti-racism in educational theory and praxis', *Discourse*, vol. 27, no. 1, 11–32.

Gillborn, D. and Mirza, H. (2000) *Educational Inequality: Mapping Race, Class and Gender*, London, Ofsted.

Giroux, H. (1992) *Border Crossings*, London, Routledge.

Gleeson, D. (1983) 'Further education, tripartism and the labour market', in Gleeson, D (ed.) *Youth Training and the Search for Work*, London, Routledge & Kegan Paul.

— (ed.) (1988) *TVEI and Secondary Education: A Critical Appraisal*, Milton Keynes, Open University Press.

— (2001) 'Style and substance in education leadership: further education (FE) as a case in point', *Journal of Education Policy*, vol. 16, no. 3, 181–96.

Gleeson, D., Davies, J. and Wheeler, E. (2005) 'On the making and taking of professionalism in the further education (FE) workplace', *British Journal of Sociology of Education*, vol. 26, no. 4, 445–60.

Gleeson, D. and Keep, E. (2004) 'Voice without accountability: the changing relationship between employers, the state and education in England', *Oxford Review of Education*, vol. 30, no. 1, 37–63.

Gleeson, D. and Mardle, G. (1980) *Further Education or Training?*, London, Routledge & Kegan Paul.

Gleeson, D. and Shain, F. (1999) 'Managing ambiguity: between markets and managerialism', *Sociological Review*, vol. 57, no. 3, 461–90.

Goldthorpe, J. H., Lockwood, D., Bechofer, F. and Platt, J. (1968a) *The Affluent Worker: Industrial Attitudes and Behaviour*, Cambridge, Cambridge University Press.

— (1968b) *The Affluent Worker: Political Attitudes and Behaviour*, Cambridge, Cambridge University Press.

— (1969) *The Affluent Worker in the Class Structure*, Cambridge, Cambridge University Press.

Gough, D. (2000) 'Evidence-informed policy and practice', Learning and Skills Agency Annual Conference, Research of the New Learning and Skills Sector, University of Warwick, 11–13 December.

Gouldner, A. (1968) *Patterns of Industrial Bureaucracy*, London, Free Press.

Grace, G. (1987) 'Teachers and the State in Britain', in Lawn, M. and Grace, G. (eds), *Teachers: The Culture and Politics of Work*, London, Falmer.

Gramsci, A. (1971) *Selections from the Prison Notebooks*, London, Lawrence & Wishart.

Griffiths, K. (2003) 'Their jobs are on the line', the *Independent*, 10 November, 4–5.

Grundy, S. (1987) *Curriculum: Product or Praxis*, Lewes, Falmer.

Guile, D. and Lucas, N. (1999) 'Rethinking initial teacher education and professional development in further education', in Green, A. and Lucas, N. (eds), *FE and Lifelong Learning*, Bedford Way Papers, London, Institute of Education.

Habermas, J. (1972) *Knowledge and Human Interest*, 2nd edn, London, Heinemann.

Haddon, L. (1983) 'The social relations of youth: a case study of the use of a further education college', unpublished MA thesis, CCCS, University of Birmingham.

Hager, P. (2000) 'Knowledge that works: judgment and the university curriculum', in Garrick, J. and Rhodes, C. (eds), *Research and Knowledge at Work*, London, Routledge.

Hall, S. (1988) *The Hard Road to Renewal: Thatcherism and the Crisis of the Left*, London, Lawrence & Wishart.

Halpin, D. (2003) *Hope and Education*, London, RoutledgeFalmer.

Halsey, A. H., Floud, J. and Anderson, C. A. (eds) (1961) *Education, Economy and Society: A Reader in the Sociology of Education*, London, Macmillan.

Ham, C. (1996) *Public, Private or Community: What Next for the NHS?*, London, Demos.

Hammersley, M. (1984) 'The paradigm mentality: a diagnosis', in Barton,

L. and Walker, S. (eds), *Social Crisis and Educational Research*, London, Croom Helm.

— (1985) 'From ethnography to theory: a programme and paradigm in the sociology of education', *Sociology*, vol. 19, no. 2, 244–59.

— (1987) 'Ethnography and the cumulative development of theory', *British Educational Research Journal*, vol. 13, no. 3, 283–96.

— (2001) 'On "systematic" reviews of research literatures: a "narrative" response to Evans and Benefield', *British Educational Research Journal*, vol. 27 no. 5, 543–54.

— (2005) 'Countering the "new orthodoxy" in educational research: a response to Phil Hodkinson', *British Educational Research Journal*, vol. 31, no. 2, 139–55.

Handy, C. (1997) 'Finding sense in uncertainty', in Gibson, R. (ed.) *Rethinking the Future*, London, Nicholas Brealey.

Hargreaves, A. (1994) *Changing Teachers, Changing Times*, London, Cassell.

— (2003) *Teaching in the Knowledge Society: Education in the Age of Insecurity*, Maidenhead, Open University Press.

Hargreaves, D. (2001) 'A capital theory of school effectiveness and improvement', *British Educational Research Journal*, vol. 27, no. 4, 487–503.

— (2003) *Education Epidemic: Transforming Secondary Schools through Innovation Networks*, London, Demos.

Harkin, J., Dawn, T. and Turner, G. (2001) *Teaching Young Adults*, London, Routledge.

Hatcher, R. (1997) 'Post-Conservative education policy: implications for social justice', paper presented to the British Educational Research Association Annual Conference, University of York, 11–14 September.

Haywood, C. and Mac an Ghail, M. (1997) '"A man in the making": sexual masculinities within changing training cultures', *The Sociological Review*, vol. 45, no. 4, 576–90.

Hayes, D., Mills, M., Christie, P. and Lingard, B. (2006), *Teachers and Schooling Making a Difference: Productive Pedagogies, Assessment and Performance*, Sydney: Allen & Unwin.

Held, D. (1980) *Introduction to Critical Theory: Horkheimer to Habermas*, Cambridge, Polity.

Henry, T. (1994) 'Changing college culture', *Coombe Lodge Reports*, vol. 24, 213–23.

Hillage, J., Pearson, R., Anderson, A. and Tamkin, P. (1998) *Excellence in Research on Schools*, London, DfEE.

HM Treasury (2004) *Skills in the Global Economy*, London, HM Treasury.

Hodge, M. (2003) 'Widening participation and fair access', speech to the Smith Institute Seminar, 21 May.

Hodgson, A. and Spours, K. (eds) (1997) *Dearing and Beyond, 14–19 Qualifications, Frameworks and Systems*, London, Kogan Page.

— (1999) *New Labour's Educational Agenda: Issues and Policies for Education and Training from 14+*, London, Kogan Page.

Hodkinson, P. (1997) 'Neo-Fordism and teacher professionalism', *Teacher Development*, vol. 1, no. 1, 69–81.

— (2004) 'Research as a form of work: expertise, community and methodological objectivity', *British Educational Research Journal*, vol. 30, no. 1, 9–26.

— (2005) 'Making improvement through research possible: the need for radical changes in the FE system', paper presented to West Yorkshire LSRN Conference, 8 July.

— (2006) 'Unfinished business', paper presented to Lifelong learning Institute, University of Leeds.

Hodkinson, P., Biesta, G., Gleeson, D., James, D. and Postlethwaite, K. (2005) 'Transforming learning cultures in further education' ESRC Research Report (abbreviated), mimeo.

Hodkinson, P. and Bloomer, M. (2000) 'Stokingham Sixth Form College: institutional culture and dispositions to learning', *British Journal of Sociology of Education*, vol. 21, no. 2, 187–202.

— (2001) 'Dropping out of further education: complex causes and simplistic policy assumptions', *Research Papers in Education*, vol. 16, no. 2, 117–40.

Hodkinson, P. and James, D. (2003) 'Introduction: transforming learning cultures in further education, *Journal of Vocational Education and Training*, vol. 55, no. 4, 389–406.

Hodkinson, P., Sparkes, A. and Hodkinson, H. (1996) *Triumph and Tears: Young People, Markets and the Transition from School to Work*, London, David Fulton.

Hollands, R. G. (1990) *The Long Transition: Class, Culture and Youth Training*, London, Macmillan.

Holmes, G. (1993) *Essential School Leadership*, London, Kogan Page.

Hughes, C. (2000) 'Is it possible to be a feminist manager in the "real world" of further education?', *Journal of Further and Higher Education*, vol. 24, no. 2, 251–60.

Hutton, W. (1995) *The State We're In*, London, Jonathan Cape.

— (1997) *The State to Come*, London, Vintage.

Hyland, T. (1994) *Competence, Education and NVQs: Dissenting Perspectives*, London, Cassell.

— (2002) 'Reconstructing modern apprentices: enhancing vocationalism through work-based learning', unpublished mimeo.

James, D. (2002) 'Towards a useful notion of learning culture', paper presented to the *British Educational Research Association Conference*, University of Exeter, 12–14 September.

— (2004) *Research in Practice: Experiences, Insights and Interventions from the Project Transforming Learning Cultures in Further Education, Building effective research: 5*, London, Learning and Skills Research Centre.

James, D. and Bloomer, M. (2001) 'Cultures of learning and the learning of cultures', paper presented to the *Cultures of Learning Conference*, University of Bristol, April.

James, D. and Diment, K. (2003) 'Going underground? Learning and assessment in an ambiguous space', *Journal of Vocational Education and Training*, vol. 55, no. 4, 407–22.

Jamieson, I. (1993) 'The rise and fall of the work-related curriculum', in Wellington, J. (ed.) *The Work-related Curriculum: Challenging the Vocational Imperative*, London, Kogan Page.

Johnson, R. (1979a) 'Unit 4 Popular politics: education and the state', Block 1 *The State and the Politics of Education*, Part 1, Milton Keynes, Open University Press.

— (1979b) '"Really useful knowledge": radical education and working-class culture, 1790–1848', in Clarke, J., Critcher, C. and Johnson, R. (eds), *Working-class Culture: Studies in History and Theory*, London, Hutchinson.

— (1998) 'Sexual emergenc(i)es: cultural theories and contemporary sexual politics' *Keywords*, vol. 1, no. 1, 74–94.

Johnson, R. and Steinberg, D. L. (2004) 'Distinctiveness and difference within New Labour', in Johnson, R. and Steinberg, D. L. (eds), *Blairism and the War of Persuasion: Labour's Passive Revolution*, London, Lawrence & Wishart.

Jones, K. (1983) *Beyond Progressive Education*, London, Macmillan.

— (2004) 'A new past, an old future: New Labour remakes the English school', in Johnson, R. and Steinberg, D. L. (eds) *Blairism and the War of Persuasion: Labour's Passive Revolution*, London, Lawrence & Wishart.

Joseph Rowntree Foundation (1995) *Inquiry into Income and Wealth*, vols 1 and 2, York, Joseph Rowntree Foundation.

JVET (*Journal of Vocational Education and Training*) (2003) 'Transforming learning cultures in further education', special issue vol. 55, no. 4.

Kay, J. (1996) *The Business of Economics*, Oxford, Oxford University Press.

Keddie, N. (1971) 'Classroom knowledge', in Young, M. F. D. (ed.) *Knowledge and Control*, Collier-Macmillan.

Keep, E. (1997) '"There's no such thing as society": some problems with an individual approach to creating a Learning Society', *Journal of Education Policy*, vol. 12, no. 6, 457–71.

— (1999) 'UK's VET policy and the third way', *Journal of Education and Work*, vol. 12, no. 3, 323–46.

Kennedy, H. (1997) *Learning Works: Widening Participation in Further Education*, Coventry, Further Education Funding Council.

Kerfoot, D. and Whitehead, S. (2000) 'Keeping all the balls in the air: further education and the masculine/managerial subject', *Journal of Further and Higher Education*, vol. 24, no. 2, 183–201.

Kingston, P. (2004) 'Education: can't pay, won't stay', the *Guardian Education*, 25 May, 2.

Kinman, G. (1996) *Occupational Stress and Health Among Lecturers Working in Further and Higher Education: A Survey Report*, London, Natfhe.

Labour Party (2004) 'Britain is working. Don't let the Tories wreck it again', www.labour.org.uk/aboutlabour/, accessed 7 December 2004.

Lacey, C. (1988) 'The idea of a socialist education', in Lauder, H. and Brown, P. (eds), *Education in Search of a Future*, London, Falmer.

Lather, P. (2003) 'This **IS** your father's paradigm: government intrusion and the case of qualitative research in education', Guba lecture, sponsored by AERA Special Interest Group: Qualitative Research, Chicago, www.coe.ohio-state.edu/plather/.

Latour, B. (1998) 'From the world of science to the world of research', in *Science*, no. 280, pp. 280–9.

Lauder, H. (2001) 'Innovation, skill diffusion, and social exclusion', in Brown, P., Green, A. and Lauder, H. (eds) (2001) *High Skills: Globalization, Competitiveness and Skill Formation*, Oxford, Oxford University Press.

Lauder, H. and Brown, P. (2003) 'Education, class and economic competitiveness', in Freeman-Moir, J. and Scott, A. (eds), *Yesterday's Dreams: International and Critical Perspectives on Education and Social Class*, Christchurch, Canterbury University Press.

Lauder, H., Brown, P. and Halsey, A. H. (2004) 'Sociology and political arithmetic', *British Journal of Sociology*, vol. 55, no. 1, 3–22.

Lave, J. and Wenger, E. (1991) *Situated Learning: Legitimate Peripheral Participation*, Cambridge, Cambridge University Press.

Lawn, M. (1988) 'Skill in schoolwork', in Ozga, J. (ed.) *Schoolwork: Approaches to the Labour Process of Teaching*, Milton Keynes, Open University Press.

— (1996) *Modern Times: Work, Professionalism and Citizenship in Teaching*, London, Falmer.

Lawton, D. (2005) *Education and the Labour Party Ideologies 1900–2001 and Beyond*, London, RoutledgeFalmer.

Lawy, R. (2003) 'Transformation of person, identity and understanding: a case study', *British Journal of Sociology of Education*, vol. 24, no. 3, 331–45.

— (2004) 'Knowledge, identity and learning in work and non-work contexts: two reflexive accounts', paper presented to the *Discourse, power and resistance Conference*, Plymouth, April 5–7.

Leadbeater, C. (1999) *Living on Thin Air*, Harmondsworth, Viking.

Leathwood, C. (2005) ' "Treat me as a human being – don't look at me as a woman": femininities and professional identities in further education', *Gender and Education*, vol. 17, no. 4, 387–409.

Leitch review of skills (2005) *Skills in the UK: The Long-term Challenge Interim Report*, Norwich, HMSO.

Leonard, P. (2000) 'Gendering change? Management, masculinity and the dynamics of incorporation', *Journal of Further and Higher Education*, vol. 24, no. 2, 71–84.

Levitas, R. (1999) *The Inclusive Society? Social Exclusion and New Labour,* London, Macmillan.

Lingard, B., Hayes, D. and Mills, M. (2003a) 'Teachers and productive pedagogies: contextualising, conceptualising, utilising, *Pedagogy, Culture and Society,* vol. 11, no. 3, 399–424.

Lingard, B., Hayes, D., Mills, M. and Christie, P. (2003b) *Leading Learning: Making Hope Practical in Schools,* Buckingham, Open University Press.

LLUK (Lifelong Learning UK) (2006) 'New professional standards: teacher/ tutor/ trainer education in the lifelong learning sector', Draft, Coventry, LLUK.

Lovell, T. (2000) 'Thinking feminism within and against Bourdieu', in Fowler, B. (ed.) *Reading Bourdieu on Society and Change,* Oxford, Blackwell.

LSC (2001) *Centres of Vocational Excellence in Further Education: The Way Ahead,* Coventry, LSC.

— (2005) *Learning and Skills: The Agenda for Change the Prospectus,* Coventry, LSC.

Lucas, N. (2004) *Teaching in Further Education,* London, Bedford Way Papers, Institute of Education.

Lumby, J. and Tomlinson, H. (2000) 'Principals speaking: managerialism and leadership in further education', *Research in Post-compulsory Education,* vol. 5, no. 2, 139–51.

Lyotard, J.-F. (1997) *The Postmodern Condition: A Report on Knowledge,* Manchester, Manchester University Press.

Mac an Ghail, M. (1999) '"New" cultures of training: emerging male (hetero)sexual identities', *British Educational Research Journal,* vol. 25, no. 4, 427–43.

MacLure, M. (2004) '"Clarity bordering on stupidity": where's the quality in systematic review?', paper presented to the *British Educational Research Association Annual Conference* UMIST, Manchester, September.

Maynard, J. and Smith, V. (2004) *A Rolling Stone Gathers No Moss Maintaining the Momentum of Action Research,* London, LSDA.

McAllister, F. (2005) *Well-being Concepts and Challenges,* London, Sustainable Development Research Network.

McCormick, J. (1994) *Citizens' Service,* London, IPPR

Menter, I., Muschamp, Y., Nicholls, P., Ozga, J. with Pollard, A. (1997) *Work and Identity in the Primary School: A Post-Fordist Analysis,* Buckingham, Open University Press.

Mizen, P. (1995) *The State, Young People and Youth Training: In and Against the Training State,* London, Mansell.

Moore, A. (2006) 'Some advantages and disadvantages in modes of formative assessment: misrecognition, "internalisation" and the influence of the "backwash" effect', paper presented to the *International Sociology of Education Conference,* London, 2–5 January.

Moore, R. (1983) 'Further education, pedagogy and production', in

Gleeson, D. (ed.) *Youth Training and the Search for Work*, London, Routledge & Kegan Paul.

Moos, M. (1979) 'Government youth training policy and its impact on further education', Occasional stencilled paper, CCCS, University of Birmingham.

Morris, A. (2002) *Building Effective Research*, London, Learning and Skills Research Centre.

Morris, E. (2001) 'Professionalism and trust: the future of teachers and teaching', a speech by the secretary of state for education to the Social Market Foundation, 12 November, London, SMF.

Mouffe, C. (1998) 'The end of politics?' *New Times* no. 141, 28 February, 6–7.

Mulgan, G. (2004) 'Demos', *Soundings*, issue 27, 95–9.

Mullins. S. (2005) 'An action research study of teaching and learning in a further education college', unpublished EdD thesis, University of Huddersfield.

Nash, R. (1999) *School Learning: Conversation with the Sociology of Education*, Palmerston North, Delta.

National Statistics Online (2006a) Gender, www.statistics.gov.uk/cci/nugget_print.asp?ID=434

— (2006b), Ethnicity and identity, www.statistics.gov.uk/cci/nugget_print.asp?ID=461

Neary, M. (2005) 'Popular education, critical pedagogy and academic activism', unpublished paper.

NERF (2001) 'Research and development for education: a national strategy consultation paper', Nottingham, National Education Research Forum.

Nickson, D., Warhurst, C., Witz, A. and Cullen, A.-M. (2001) 'The importance of being aesthetic: work, employment and service organisation', in Sturdy, A., Grugulis, I. and Willmott, H. (eds), *Customer Service: Empowerment and Entrapment*, London, Palgrave.

Nixon, J. (2001) 'Not without dust and heat': the moral bases of the new academic professionalism', *British Journal of Educational Studies*, vol. 49, no. 2, 173–86.

Nixon, J., Marks, A., Rowland, S. and Walker, M. (2001) 'Towards a new academic professionalism: a manifesto of hope', *British Journal of Sociology of Education*, vol. 22, no. 2, 227–44.

Nixon, J. and Ranson, S. (1997) 'Theorising agreement: the moral basis of the emergent professionalism within the new management of education', *Discourse*, vol. 18, no. 2, 197–214.

Nowotny, H., Scott, P. and Gibbons, M. (2002) *Re-thinking Science: Knowledge and the Public in an Age of Uncertainty*, Cambridge, Polity.

Oakley, A. (2000) *Experiments in Knowing: Gender and Method in the Social Sciences*, Cambridge, Polity.

— (2002) 'Social science and evidence-based everything: the case of education', *Educational Review*, vol. 54, no. 3, 277–86.

Olssen M. (2003) 'Structuralism, post-structuralism, neo-liberalism: assessing Foucault's legacy', *Journal of Education Policy*, vol. 18, no. 2, 189–202.

Olssen, M., Codd, J. and O'Neil, A.-M. (2004) *Education Policy, Globalization, Citizenship and Democracy*, London, Sage.

Ozga, J. (1990) 'Policy research and policy theory', *Journal of Education Policy*, vol. 5, no. 4, 359–62.

Ozga, J. and Lawn, M. (1981) *Teachers, Professionalism and Class*, London, Falmer.

Preston, J. (2003) 'White trash vocationalism? Formations of class and race in an Essex further education college', *Widening Participation and Lifelong Learning*, vol. 5, no. 2, 6–17.

Pring, R. (2000) *Philosophy of Educational Research*, London, Continuum.

Randle, K. and Brady, N. (1997a) 'Managerialism and professionalism in the "Cinderella Service"', *Journal of Vocational Education and Training*, vol. 49, no. 1, 121–40.

— (1997b) 'Further education and the new managerialism', *Journal of Further and Higher Education*, vol. 21, no. 2, 229–38.

Ranson, S. (2003) 'Public accountability in the age of neo-liberal governance', *Journal of Education Policy*, vol. 18, no. 5, 459–80.

Ranson, S. and Stewart, J. (1998) 'The Learning Democracy' in Ranson, S. (ed.) *Inside the Learning Society*, London, Cassell.

Reay, D. (2003) 'Reproduction, reproduction, reproduction', in Freeman-Moir, J. and Scott, A. (eds), *Yesterday's Dreams: International and Critical Perspectives on Education and Social Class*, Christchurch, Canterbury University Press.

Reay, D., Davis, M. and Ball, S, (2005) *Degrees of Choice: Social Class, Race and Gender in Higher Education*, Stoke-on-Trent, Trentham.

Reich, R. (1991) *The Work of the Nations: A Blueprint for the Future*, London, Simon & Schuster.

Renewal (2006) vol. 14, no. 1.

Rikowski, G. (1999) 'Education, capital and the transhuman', in Hill, D., MacLaren, P., Cole, M. and Rikowski, G. (eds), *Postmodernism in Educational Theory: Education and the Politics of Human Resistance*, London, Tufnell.

Rikowski, G. (2001) 'Education for industry: a complex technicism', *Journal of Education and Work*, vol. 14, no. 1, 29–49.

Robertson, D. (1994) 'Flexibility and mobility in further and higher education: policy continuity and progress', *Journal of Further and Higher Education*, vol. 17, no. 1, 68–79.

Robson, J. (2002) 'The voices of vocational teachers in the UK: their perceptions of the nature and status of the further education teachers' professional knowledge', *Australian and New Zealand Journal of Vocational Education Research*, vol. 10, no. 2, 95–113.

Rose, N. (1999) 'Inventiveness in politics', *Economy and Society*, vol. 28, no. 3, 467–93.

Rustin, M. (1997) 'Editorial: what next?', *Soundings*, special issue, 'The next ten Years', 7–18.

Sachs, J. (2003a) *The Activist Teaching Profession*, Maidenhead, Open University Press.

— (2003b) 'Teacher activism: mobilising the profession', plenary address presented to the British Educational Research Association Conference, Heriot Watt University, Edinburgh, 11–13 September, Southwell.

Savage, M. (2003) 'A new class paradigm', *British Journal of Sociology of Education*, vol. 24, no. 4, 535–41.

Scheeres, H. and Solomon, N. (2000) 'Research partnerships at work: new identities, new times', in Garrick, J. and Rhodes, C. (eds), *Research and Knowledge at Work*, London, Routledge.

Seddon, T. (1997) 'Education: deprofessionalised? Or reregulated, reorganised and reauthorised?', *Australian Journal of Education*, vol. 41, no. 3, 228–46.

Sennett, R. (2006) *The Culture of the New Capitalism*, New Haven, Yale University Press.

Shah, H. and Marks, N. (2004) *A Well-being Manifesto for a Flourishing Society*, London, New Economics Foundation.

Shain, F. and Gleeson, D. (1999) 'Under new management: changing conceptions of teacher professionalism and policy in the further education sector, *Journal of Educational Policy*, vol. 14, no. 4, 445–62.

Sharp, R. and Green, A. (1975) *Education and Social Control*, London, Routledge & Kegan Paul.

Shilling, C, (1988) *Schooling for Work in Capitalist England*, Lewes, Falmer.

Simkins, T. and Lumby, J. (2002) 'Cultural transformation in further education? Mapping the debate', *Research in Post-compulsory Education*, vol. 7, no. 1, 9–25.

Simmons, R. (2006) 'Revisiting Braverman: the labour process in further education', unpublished mimeo.

Skeggs, B. (1988) 'Gender reproduction and further education', *British Journal of Sociology of Education*, vol. 9, no. 2, 131–49.

— (1991) 'Challenging masculinity and using sexuality', *British Journal of Sociology of Education*, vol. 12, no. 2, 127–40.

— (1997) *Formation of Class and Gender*, London, Sage.

Smith, A. M. (1994) *New Right Discourse on Race and Sexuality*, Cambridge, Cambridge University Press.

Smith, A. and Webster, F. (1997) 'Conclusion: an affirming flame', in Smith, A. and Webster, F. (eds), *The Postmodern University? Contested Visions of Higher Education in Society*, Buckingham, Open University Press.

Social Exclusion Unit (1999) *Bridging the Gap: New Opportunities for 16–18 year olds Not in Education, Employment or Training* Cm 4405, London, Cabinet Office.

Social Trends (2006) vol. 36, London, HMSO.

Solihull College (undated) 'Research policy', unpublished mimeo.

Stafford, A. (1991) *Trying Work: Gender, Youth and Work Experience*, Edinburgh, Edinburgh University Press.

Stronach, I., Corbin, B., McNamara, O., Stark, S. and Warne, T. (2002) 'Towards an uncertain politics of professionalism', *Journal of Educational Policy*, vol. 17, no. 1, 109–38.

Symes, C. and McIntyre, J. (eds) (2000a) *Working Knowledge: The New Vocationalism and Higher Education*, Buckingham, Open University Press.

THES (*The Times Higher Education Supplement*) (2002–6), various issues.

Thomas, G. and Pring, R. (2004) *Evidence-based Practice in Education*, Buckingham, Open University Press.

Thompson, P. and Lawson, N. (2006) 'Putting class back into British politics', *Renewal*, vol. 14, no. 1, 1–7.

Thrupp, M. and Wilmott, R. (2004) *Education Management in Managerialist Times: Beyond the Textual Apologists*, Maidenhead, Open University Press.

Tomlinson Report (2004) *14–19 Curriculum and Qualifications Reform: Final Report of the Working Group on 14–19 Reform*, Annesley, DfES.

Tomorrow project (undated) 'What might be the implication?' www.tomorrowproject.net/pub/pub/1_GLIMPSES/documents/N234+.html, accessed 19 April 2006.

Tooley, J. and Darby, D. (1998) *Educational Research: A Critique*, London, Ofsted.

Unwin, L. (1997) 'Teacher as researcher: collaborative approaches and distance learning', in Robson, J. (ed.) *The Professional FE Teacher*, Aldershot, Avebury.

Unwin, L. and Wellington, J. (2001) *Young People's Perspectives on Education, Training and Employment: Realizing their Potential*, London, Kogan Page.

Venables, E. (1967) *The Young Worker at College*, London, Faber & Faber.

— (1974) *Apprentices Out of Their Time*, London, Faber & Faber.

Viskovic, A. and Robson, J. (2001) 'Community and identity: experiences and dilemmas of vocational teachers in post-school contexts', *Journal of In-service Education*, vol. 27, no. 2, 221–36.

Walhberg, M. and Gleeson, D. (2003) '"Doing the business": paradox and irony in vocational education', *Journal of Vocational Education and Training*, vol. 55, no. 4, 423–46.

Warhurst, C., Grugulis, I. and Keep, E. (eds) (2004) *The Skills that Matter*, London, Palgrave.

Warmington, P. (2003) '"You need a qualification for everything these days": the impact of work, welfare and disaffection upon the aspirations of access to higher education students', *British Journal of Sociology of Education*, vol. 24, no. 1, 95–108.

White, D. (2003)' India answers the call of prosperity', the *Daily Telegraph*, 8 November, p. 32.

Whitmarsh, J. (2005) 'Real mothers: real lives', unpublished PhD, University of Wolverhampton.

Williams, R. (1973) *The Long Revolution*, Harmondsworth, Penguin.

Willis, P. (1977) *Learning to Labour: How Working-Class Kids get Working-class Jobs*, Farnborough, Saxon House.

— (2004) 'Twenty-five years on: old books, new times', in Dolby, N., Dimitriadis, G. and Willis, P. (2004) *Learning to labour in New Times*, London RoutledgeFalmer.

Wilkinson, R. (2006) 'The impact of inequality: the empirical evidence', *Renewal*, vol. 14, no. 1, 20–6.

Wolf, A. (2002) *Does Education Matter? Myths about Education and Economic Growth*, London, Penguin.

Woods, P. and Jeffrey, B. (2002) 'The reconstruction of primary teachers' identities', *British Journal of Sociology of Education*, vol. 23, no. 1, 89–106.

Youdell, D. (2003) 'Identity traps or how black students fail: the interaction between biographical, subcultural, and learner identities', *British Journal of Sociology of Education*, vol. 24, no. 1, 3–20.

Young, M. F. D. (ed.) (1971) *Knowledge and control, new directions for the sociology of education*, London: Collier Macmillan.

— (1977) 'Curriculum change: limits and possibilities', in Young, M. and Whitty, G. (eds), *Society, State and Schooling*, Ringmer, Falmer.

— (1993) 'A curriculum for the 21st century?', *British Journal of Educational Studies*, vol. 41, no. 3, 203–22.

— (1998a) *The Curriculum of the Future: From the 'New Sociology of Education' to a Critical Theory of Learning*, London, Falmer.

— (1998b) 'Post-compulsory education for a learning society', in Ranson, S. (ed.) *Inside the Learning Society*, London, Cassell.

— (1999) 'Knowledge, learning and the curriculum of the future', an inaugural lecture, London, Institute of Education.

— (2001) 'Contextualising a new approach to learning: some comments on Yrjo Engeström's theory of expansive learning', *Journal of Education and Work*, vol. 14, no. 1, 157–61.

— (2003) 'Durkheim, Vygotsky and the curriculum of the future', *London Review of Education*, vol. 1, no. 2, 99–117.

— (2004) 'An old problem in a new context: rethinking the relationship between sociology and educational policy', in *International Studies in Sociology of Education*, vol. 14, no. 1, 3–20.

Young, M. and Spours, K. (1997) 'Unifying academic and vocational learning and the idea of the learning society', *Journal of Education Policy*, vol. 12, no. 6, 527–37.

Young, M. and Whitty, G. (eds) (1977) *Society, State and Schooling*, Ringmer, Falmer.

Index